TREASURE HOARDS

of East Anglia
and their Discovery

Mark Mitchels

COUNTRYSIDE BOOKS
NEWBURY BERKSHIRE

First published 2009
© Mark Mitchels 2009

COUNTRYSIDE BOOKS
3 Catherine Road
Newbury, Berkshire

To view our complete range of books,
please visit us at
www.countrysidebooks.co.uk

*To my wonderful and long-suffering family,
who have had to endure my obsession
with all things historical*

ISBN 978 1 84674 147 0

Cover picture of coins from the
Sedgeford Gallo-Belgic hoard
supplied by Susan James

Designed by Peter Davies, Nautilus Design
Produced through MRM Associates Ltd., Reading
Printed by Information Press, Oxford

Contents

Introduction

East Anglia is an excellent place to set a book about treasure hoards, because there is probably nowhere else in the British Isles that has produced richer discoveries of international importance. The stories behind such fabulous finds are worth retelling, although I must apologize for the frequent use of words like *probably, possibly, perhaps, maybe* and others which allow me to confess ignorance of the crucial historical details, now lost in antiquity!

The metal detector has transformed archaeology and, after a delay, the law has caught up with it. The Treasure Act 1996 has simplified the law and provided an incentive for responsible metal detectorists to work with local archaeologists. It is encouraging how many of the important discoveries in this book show how successful the Act has been – but, of course, less honest searches remain unknown! An outline code of conduct is included at the end of this book.

While I have frequently commented on the value given to the treasure at the time of its discovery, I have not attempted to give modern equivalents. In some cases the contemporary figure is truly astonishing.

As you read, I hope you are encouraged to visit these treasures where they are displayed. The British Museum, at times, may appear to hoover up all the best material but, in fairness, that is where the experts are based, and it has the resources to display them to perfection to the largest number of people. The regional museums in Norwich, Cambridge, Ipswich, Chelmsford and Colchester have wonderful collections, and usually include loans from the British Museum too. Some of the local museums in the region provide really outstanding presentations of their own materials and bring to the topic an enthusiasm which is very exciting. It would be unfair to single out only a few, but I must mention Mildenhall, Thetford and March, at least!

For those readers who enjoy using a metal detector just consider this: it is entirely possible that one day – tomorrow? – you might just find the next great treasure hoard!

Good luck, and make sure you follow the rules or the rewards may pass you by!

Mark Mitchels

Acknowledgements

Grateful thanks to the staff of the British Museum, Ipswich and Colchester Museums, Norwich Castle Museum and Chelmsford Museum for permission to use material from their collections. Where possible, I have indicated the picture sources, but if there are any contraventions of copyright I offer my apologies and promise to correct any errors in later editions.

THE SNETTISHAM GOLD

In 1948 a tractor passed between the gate posts at the entrance of Ken Hill, at Snettisham in Norfolk, and the driver prepared for yet another day's ploughing. He had been given instructions to plough deeper than usual, but at the time he probably thought nothing of it. Soon he was working his way across the field. At one point he glanced across to a previous furrow and his attention was caught by something which caused him to stop, dismount and walk over to the spot. He bent down, picked up something metallic, rubbed it with his hand and then paused to study it. Whatever it was, it hardly seemed to belong in a windswept field, so he took it back to the tractor, stowed it under the seat and went on with his work.

A short while later, he observed the foreman waiting for him at the end of the track. He drew up beside him, made a brief report, and then remembered the lump of metal. With a dismissive comment, he tossed the earth-encrusted shape to the foreman, who turned it over in his hands, spat on it, rubbed it and pronounced it to be part of a brass bedstead. With a laugh he threw it down beside the hedge, and the two men parted. Soon the tractor was once again making its lonely way across the field and the 'bedstead' was forgotten.

Several days later, the tractor was still at work in the field, this time breaking down the massive banks of soil to prepare them for sowing. The driver had forgotten all about the find he had made, but remembered it when he saw some more bits of metal on the ground, in almost the same spot. This time he could make out coin-shaped objects, and some bracelets, all of them caked in mud, but beneath they were bright and appeared in good condition. He searched the area for a while and found a few more.

NORWICH CASTLE MUSEUM HAS A FINE DISPLAY OF TORCS FROM
SNETTISHAM. THIS ONE DEMONSTRATES THE CRAFTSMANSHIP OF THE
UNKNOWN GOLDSMITH. (*Norwich Castle Museum*)

Satisfied he had collected all that were to be discovered, he returned to his
tractor and carried on work.

At the end of the day he showed them to the farmer, who immediately
recognized them as being of gold. When they were given the most basic clean
they were revealed as objects of great craftsmanship and in almost perfect
condition. The farmer contacted Norwich Museum, where Mr Rainbow
Clark examined them and pronounced them to be Celtic gold torcs.

It was at this point that the driver remembered the 'bedstead' fragment at the edge of the field, and set off to recover it. Sure enough, it too was gold and even larger than the pieces he had found already. They now had five gold torcs, a fabulous discovery and soon to be a cause of great excitement throughout the world of archaeology.

Torc is ultimately derived from the Latin *torquere* 'to twist', and torcs feature a number of wires twisted together, rather like rope or electric cable, with terminals at the end which are both functional and extravagantly grand. Of all the items which survive from the Iron Age, torcs are the most charged with symbolism. They are to be found across the pre-Roman world of north-west Europe and in every case they had clearly acquired importance beyond their gold or silver content. They represented the height of the craftsman's skill and were imbued with sacred status.

There are no written records to tell us how torcs were worn. The design of a torc means that it can easily be placed around the neck or wrist. A twisting movement enables the wearer to slip it on or off.

The law required that there should be a Treasure Trove inquest to determine ownership of the torcs found at Snettisham, and, at its conclusion, the farmer received a substantial reward, and the torcs were removed to Norwich for cleaning and display. For 2,000 years they had lain beneath the soil of Ken Hill and now they were experiencing the light of day once more.

Perhaps there were more to be found? Indeed there were.

Throughout the 1950s and 1960s the field at Snettisham continued to produce more torcs and other Celtic metal work. The finest, the Great Torc, is seen by many as the glory of the Celtic age. Other finds were less exciting, but no less interesting. It was clear that, in addition to hoards of gold and silver, which included rings and coins, there were also accumulations of scrap metal, and even collections of broken and repaired jewellery. Not all were gold or silver. There was a quantity made of electrum, which is an alloy of gold and silver with bronze added, which makes it much easier to work into jewellery. Obviously it is impossible to put a precise date to the coins, as they do not obligingly have dates on them, but the experts at that time were satisfied that the approximate date of burial was 87-85 BC, which is impressively specific for anything of this period.

Sir Stephen Green was the owner of Ken Hill in the 1970s and he provides an amusing counter to the idea that almost anyone could walk across the field and find a piece of archaeological treasure. He told how one day he gathered all his workers together and brought to the field every plough he could find. As the machines scraped their way across, the workers followed, intently scanning the furrows, looking for any traces of metal. After a long, tedious session which took in the entire field what had they found? Nothing! He recalled that soon afterwards the BBC turned up. They were filming a documentary and had hopes of the cameras being there when exciting discoveries were made. What happened? They found nails by the dozen and bits of old farm machinery. Nothing else. Perhaps at last the field was exhausted? It was not.

A week later a farm worker was guiding his tractor across Ken Hill, dressing the soil with fertilizer, when he spotted an empty plastic bag trapped in a furrow. Curious, and keen to tidy up a mess, he got down from his cab and picked it up. Guess what he found underneath the bag? A gold torc! And that was not the last by any means. A young driver noticed something was fouling up one of the seed drills and, sure enough, he had found yet another torc.

A FIELD AT SNETTISHAM WHERE TORCS AND OTHER TREASURES WERE DISCOVERED OVER SEVERAL DECADES.

In 1989 metal detecting equipment was available, and a new hobby had been created. For many families, the problem of what to buy someone for Christmas had been solved! Unfortunately, the ownership of the kit did not convey the right to scour another's property, or claim rights of ownership to whatever was dug up. A sort of monster had been created, and it was not welcomed by the archaeological community. But from the beginning, there were polite and responsible detectorists (as they are known) and Ken Hill was about to meet one.

Charles Hodder asked permission of the Snettisham Estate to search the fields with his metal detector in 1989, and permission was given. For many months he walked his lonely vigil, sweeping the soil, alert for that tell-tale change of pulse in his headphones. There was little to excite him at first, just fragments and a couple of gold coins, but he hit the jackpot on 25 August 1990 – Bank Holiday Monday.

He identified a bronze container, which seemed to be full of scrap metal, although it was far from easy to interpret. As it was the Bank Holiday, he knew there was not much chance of an archaeologist being available on call, so he decided to have a go at uncovering it himself. To have walked away, leaving the hole open, was not an option for a sensible detectorist. When he had exposed the contents of the pot he found himself looking at a strange sight: here was a hoard of precious metal waiting to be melted down, and recast as something else. Or maybe not, for it had been buried quite deliberately. The mystery of Snettisham had deepened.

The significance of Charles Hodder's discovery was not lost on Dr Ian Stead, Deputy Keeper of Prehistoric and Romano-British Antiquities at the British Museum. On his arrival he realised the story of Ken Field had taken an exciting turn. The deep-ploughing discoveries had all apparently been made, but here was a new technique which could reveal the truth of what lurked even further down.

The subsequent British Museum excavation was extremely thorough. They cleared about a quarter of an acre using trowels, scraping away the soil until they located the natural soil, which had never been disturbed. But evidence of Iron Age occupation or use was missing. Not exactly desperate, but certainly puzzled, they decided to excavate the field in an unusual way. They brought in a box scraper, attached it to the back of a tractor, and simply took off the soil in impressive sweeps. And quite literally, on the last day allocated for excavation, they found treasure.

They found five pits, each containing torcs of various types, and in differing states of repair and workmanship. Three pits were of particular interest to them, as they plainly showed the care with which the deposits were made. The pits seemed to have been given two levels. In one of them, the upper level contained a nest of seven silver and bronze torcs. But in the corner of this pit was evidence of another hole, and this led to an even greater discovery. The lower pit contained two bronze bracelets, then two silver torcs, and, at the very lowest point in the pit, ten perfect gold torcs. It must have been a moment to savour for the archaeologists.

The three double-pits and their stratified treasures really permitted only one interpretation: the people who buried them had deliberately sought to confuse anyone who found the torcs. The earth layer between them was intended to satisfy careless diggers and prevent them from learning of the even greater riches beneath.

Incredibly, the hoards of Snettisham cannot be assumed to be exhausted. To date they comprise 180 torcs of various sorts and in all sorts of conditions, 100 ingots of precious metals, various rings and such like, and well over 200 gold and silver coins.

Charles Hodder had made a great discovery and had led the archaeologists to others. But he responsibly only claimed Treasure Trove on his first one and received the generous reward from the State to which he was entitled. His exceptionally responsible attitude towards his find, in that he informed the authorities at the first opportunity, and left the evidence in place, was of enormous importance in the story of modern archaeology. For the first time in the United Kingdom archaeologists were able to examine a detectorist's finds in context. Even more significantly, the entire centuries-old concept of Treasure Trove was found to be wanting in the age of the metal detector and, in due course, the law would be changed directly as a result of these events. Snettisham had earned another place in the history books.

A team from the British Museum worked at Ken Hill in 1991, scraping yet more soil to the side and, while they did not make any more spectacular discoveries, they did find quantities of iron slag in a ditch, indicating that metal working actually took place on site at some period in its story. A magnetometer survey enabled the experts to claim the existence of a vast circular ditch, some 20 acres in extent. This was found to be later in date than the torcs suggested, and it was likely, from pottery evidence from the ditch, that the site was occupied by the Romans within a century of the conquest. But there is no suggestion that there was ever a proper settlement there, or even buildings which could have once formed part of a temple complex.

There was a time when historians believed that the Snettisham torcs were buried, perhaps in 54 BC, by refugees from Caesar's army. This idea of the 'flight hoard' was undermined when the coins were studied again. As they were familiar from other, documented, sites, an earlier date of perhaps 70 BC was suggested. This being so, the reason for their burial had nothing to do with the Romans.

That still left a few more possibilities. Perhaps they were evidence of a 'prehistoric treasury', a sort of bank in the middle of a field, where valuable tribal items could be hidden for safety. The lack of buildings or occupation makes this less convincing. There is also a problem in that it is difficult to imagine such a site staying a secret for long, and certainly not for several generations.

More interesting is the idea that Snettisham represents a religious centre, a place thought to possess special powers or significance in the tribal culture. Its location, on relatively high ground and just two miles from the Wash, allows it to offer a vantage point over the land of a people who understood it in all its moods and forms. The ceremonies associated with such people probably included the wearing of robes and jewellery on special occasions, and may well have required that, at times chosen by the leaders, some treasures should be placed beneath the ground to please their gods. This type of ceremony can include the deliberate destruction of items, and some of the torcs were clearly broken before being buried.

Rather less dramatic, some experts wonder whether Snettisham was not just a sort of factory where items of gold and silver were brought for repair, or even for recasting into fresh jewellery. It would explain the masses of scrap metal, but it is unlikely that such a site would be superimposed on one where fabulous items of value were patently being preserved forever. The fact is we shall never know what the purpose of the site was, but that does not prevent us from having a guess!

To the people of Iron Age Britain the gods were all-important. They controlled the seasons, harvests and climate and influenced every aspect of their lives. Failure to please them could result in catastrophe, so a priestly class evolved to interpret and organize the rituals on which their very lives depended. There would be sacred places and times of the year

OVER 180 TORCS AND OTHER TREASURES HAVE BEEN FOUND IN THE FIELDS OF SNETTISHAM. (*Norwich Castle Museum*)

when they were visited. Not all these sites needed to be possessed of stone circles, buildings or even ditches. It was enough that they were known and respected. In times of great uncertainty or danger, the gods would protect and guide, such was their power. The burial of the torcs could have been a moment when the people sought the protection of the gods. But there were also rituals which belonged in the routine of the tribal year – times to express their gratitude for prosperity and security. There were Celtic festivals called Imbolc, Leghnasa, Semain and Beltain. The last named frequently took place on hill tops and involved fire and sacrifice. At such times the people would place items of value or special significance in the soil for the gods to use. Some societies took such objects and broke them before placing them in the ground. It was just a variation of the ritual.

A leading archaeologist, Professor Barry Cunliffe, has no doubt that the Snettisham hoards were placed in the ground as part of a ritual. He is not troubled by the apparent lack of features or structures around it, commenting that it is an example of a 'natural sacred place implied by certain of the classical texts'. Snettisham, he writes, was perhaps 'little more than a clearing in a forest protected only by its sanctity and religious taboos restraining the people'.

In 1968 at Belstead, near Ipswich, another hoard was discovered. A mechanical digger was at work creating the site for a housing development. As it went to and fro, the driver's eye was caught by the light bouncing off objects his bucket had unearthed. He climbed down, examined the objects and reached a conclusion that was hopelessly wide of the mark. He assumed they were brass coffin handles and prepared to throw them on the spoil heap. Then, at the last moment, an alarm sounded in his head – why were they untarnished, and looking brand new? Just in time he realised that they were made of gold – a rare piece of coffin furniture indeed!

In the course of time the digger driver heard that the Coroner's Court had decided that this was Treasure Trove, and he received £45,000. The five torcs themselves, each about 7 inches in circumference, were 90% gold and 10% silver. Apparently the quality of metal varies depending on the time of manufacture, and this particular metal combination suggests that they were made a generation before Caesar's invasions. The Belstead torcs, with their intricate terminals, were outstanding examples of the craftsman's skill.

And there the story should end – but it does not. A year later the first proud house owners moved onto the estate, and while they were excited to be lord of all they surveyed, that did not include the heap of topsoil left behind by the builders! One man, grumbling no doubt as he did so, began to shift the mound, only to find yet another torc, for which he received £9,000 when it too was proclaimed Treasure Trove. These items may now be viewed at the British Museum.

COINS OF CUNOBELIN

Imagine that one day, perhaps as evening fell, a young man set off on an important journey. He carried with him a pot full to the brim of coins, both Celtic and Roman, although he would have been grateful that the Romans were people he had only ever heard about, and never seen. The trackway was narrow and uneven, which was unfortunate as he needed all his attention just to keep the pot of coins upright in his hands. The wind blowing his cloak around his face did not help much either. All around him stretched the fenland wastes, great black shapes of water surrounded by madly waving grasses. He looked up for a fraction too long, missed his footing and plunged off the path into the inky waters.

In 1959 a labourer called William Mackender was ploughing to a depth of about 9 inches – deeper than usual – and discovered an upturned pot. He picked it up and a cascade of coins showered to the ground. He took them to the landowner, Lady Grace Briscoe, and together they returned to search for more. By the conclusion of their efforts they had found 481 coins, both Celtic and Roman. The documented finds include 32 Iceni coins and 23 Roman ones. We shall never know the true value of what was in the pot because local people had been finding coins for years and had sold them when occasion required. A year later, in 1960, the young man who had been carrying the coins was himself unearthed, at Joist Fen, west of Lakenheath. He was now a mere skeleton in the peat bog, and had been there since just before the Roman invasion of AD 43. The coins can be seen in the Fitzwilliam Museum, Cambridge.

In 1997, nearly 50 years after the first discovery of the Snettisham gold, a metal detectorist from Southend, named Greg Newitt, was exploring land in Great Leighs, Essex, when he made a remarkable find. He unearthed

SOME OF THE GOLD IRON AGE COINS
FOUND AT GREAT LEIGHS. THE HORSE
DESIGN IS EASILY VISIBLE.
(Chelmsford Museum)

40 gold Iron Age Celtic coins called staters, which had been made in France or Belgium in the first century BC.

The Iceni are among the first tribes mentioned by the Romans and, at about the time when Julius Caesar carried out his first invasion in 55 BC, they appear to have imitated the Roman currency. Iceni coins always have a horse in some form or other on one side, which was a special animal to them, to the extent that they did not work them in the fields. The majority of the coins discovered by Greg Newitt were single-sided, all with the familiar horse design, which we now recognize as deriving from Britain. As they date from the time of Julius Caesar's campaigns in Gaul, it is thought they may have been payment to the Celtic warriors who fought him, and then somehow they made their way back over the Channel. The coins were sold for £40,000 to the Chelmsford and Essex Museum, where they are on display.

For such a varied hoard to be found together is most unusual. A year later, in 1998, Greg Newitt found eleven more coins, this time worth £8,000. He and his metal detector have not finished contributing to this story either.

Caesar's legions landed on the beach at Walmer, Kent, in 55 BC, when they were met by thousands of chariots, and they departed from Britain after a very brief campaign. Caesar's second invasion in 54 BC was a bigger, more thoroughly mounted affair. Following the lessons learned the year before, it was centred on the southern part of East Anglia, encouraged by the king of the Trinovantes tribe, who lived in Essex and the Thames valley, the richest part of Britain. The Trinovantes were constantly threatened by the neighbouring Catuvellauni tribe and their king Cassivellaunus, whose capital is believed to have been near present-day St Albans.

Cassivellaunus was pursued to his lair – probably Wheathampstead, west of St Albans – and there was obliged to surrender to Caesar. Hostages were handed over, words of submission were spoken and Caesar gratefully returned to Gaul, having won what he could claim was another triumph. But in fact he had achieved very little, and the Trinovantes had only delayed their inevitable conquest by the Catuvellauni.

By about AD 10 the Catuvellauni were led by the mighty Cunobelin and he not only conquered the Trinovantes, he appropriated their capital too and moved his power there. The Romans called it Camulodunum, and we know it as Colchester.

Cunobelin was no fool, and he maintained good relations with Rome, supplying them with British exports: grain, iron, hides, slaves and hunting dogs. The historian Suetonius refers to him as *Britannorum rex* – king of the whole province of Britain. He would have appreciated that.

Just to the west of Colchester is Lexden, and it was there in 1924 that the story of Cunobelin may have been completed. Archaeologists excavated a Bronze Age barrow, 1.5 metres high, 30 metres in diameter and surrounded by a deep ditch. During the Iron Age it had been reopened and used for a grand funeral, including a gold chain-mail tunic, weapons, and a medallion of the Emperor Augustus. From all we know of Cunobelin, it is entirely possible he would have received such a token of friendship from a Roman emperor. Some items of metalwork had been deliberately broken as part of the burial rites. A cremation had taken place and from the accompanying pottery it was possible to infer a date of about AD 40-43. In all probability, this was the last resting place of Cunobelin, otherwise known as Shakespeare's Cymbeline (or even Old King Cole of the nursery rhyme!).

Greg Newitt, who lives in Southend, was working at Great Waltham in 1998 when he had the good fortune to discover ten Iron Age gold staters, which showed the stylised horse which appears on so many coins of this period. They also show the ear of corn which proclaims the source of the region's prosperity. In 1999 Greg was again working at Great Waltham and he found yet more gold coins. The majority of them bore the name 'Cunobelin'. They were in excellent condition and, on one side, beneath a two horse chariot called a biga, was the name CVNO – Cunobelin, while on the other was the familiar ear of corn and the word CAMVL – Camulodunum. The coins were acquired by Chelmsford and Essex Museum in 2003 for £12,000.

In the spring of 2008 a metal detectorist (who modestly wishes to remain anonymous) was searching a field near Wickham Market in Suffolk when he found a coin. Soon he had uncovered a hoard of gold coins still contained within an earthenware pot. A joint excavation by Suffolk County Council and the British Museum later in the year produced a total of 825 gold coins. They appear to date from before AD 15. Two thirds of them show the familiar Iceni horse on one side but, unusually, the reverse shows a double moon emblem. It is possible they were an offering to a Celtic deity. Research on the hoard has only just begun and it will be some time before it is displayed.

JUST A FEW OF THE IRON AGE STATERS FOUND ON PASTURE LAND AT DALLINGHOO, SUFFOLK, IN THE SPRING OF 2008. THE COINS DATE FROM 40 BC TO AD 15 AND PROBABLY BELONGED TO THE ICENI TRIBE. THEY COMPRISE GOLD BUT WERE DEGRADED WITH COPPER. *(Suffolk County Council Archaeological Service)*

REBELLION & RICHES

The third Roman invasion, under Emperor Claudius, was hardly unexpected. Apart from Julius Caesar's visits almost a century earlier, the tribes of the south had known that the eye of Rome was upon them. There had even been cancelled invasions, but in AD 43 it was inevitable. In Boulogne was an army of four legions, all veterans of long, savage campaigns on the German frontier. With its many units of auxiliaries, the army numbered in the region of 40,000 men. Led by a tough, experienced commander called Aulus Plautius, it was prepared for anything the Britons could offer.

By the time the legions crossed the Thames, victory required them only to march eastwards and take the tribal capital, Colchester. But Emperor Claudius had given strict instructions and he was not about to be denied his victory. His general waited while Emperor Claudius travelled from Rome, crossed the Channel and came at last to East Anglia. He brought elephants with him, which must have suitably awed the natives! Six months later he returned to Rome and enjoyed the military triumph he was awarded.

In Colchester Museum there is a coin from this moment in history. It was struck by Claudius on his return to Rome, and shows the Triumphal Arch he built there in AD 52. He is described as *Claudius of the Britons*.

Just west of Ely is the village of Witcham, where a Roman cavalry helmet was found a long time ago. It was recovered from a gravel pit, and was in a remarkable state of preservation. It dates from the period of the Iceni revolt, and, although made mainly of bronze, it is lined with iron, and has the familiar cheek pieces and the guards for forehead and neck. There are even small bosses on the neck guard to deflect weapon blows. It shows the quality of equipment available to the soldiers of Rome, and suggests the impression they would have had on their enemies. With their discipline and tactics, they must have appeared like machines in battle.

If the Romans thought that by occupation they had subdued the tribes, they were in for a surprise. The first Iceni revolt, of AD 47, took place in what we know as Cambridgeshire, and there is evidence that a key moment of the campaign occurred close to where the helmet was found, at a place called Stonea, near March. The Iceni hill fort at Stonea is described as 'the lowest hill fort in Britain', as it sits on a layer of gravel just two metres above the water level. Here the Iceni made their stand, and the Roman army fought a fierce battle to capture it. A grisly reminder of the attack was discovered when the site was excavated. It is the skull of a small child, cleft by a mighty sword blow.

A ROMAN CAVALRY HELMET FOUND AT WITCHAM, NEAR ELY. IT WAS MADE OF BRONZE AND LINED WITH IRON.
(British Museum)

The Witcham helmet is probably a relic of the campaign. Now it is part of the British Museum collection. The remains of the destroyed ramparts and ditches can be visited today, and provide one of the most unusual and pleasant sites in East Anglia, defended only by inquisitive sheep!

Within a decade of the Conquest there were many soldiers no longer fit for duty, and so ready for retirement. The Romans had an answer to this problem. They created a *colonia*, a city for retired soldiers, where veterans could live out their days in their final posting, while at the same time demonstrating the virtues of civilisation to the rough natives. The site of the first *colonia* was at modern-day Colchester. Unfortunately, the site chosen was on land at Gosbecks, which was sacred to the Trinovantes. It was inevitable there would be trouble.

When Prasutagus, king of the Iceni, died, he thoughtfully made the Emperor his co-heir, along with his two daughters, thereby hoping to avoid an outright take-over. He could not have reckoned on the greed and contempt of the Procurator in Colchester, as the historian Tacitus explains: 'his widow Boudicca was flogged and their daughters raped. The Icenian chiefs were deprived of their hereditary estates as if the Romans had been given the whole country. The king's own relatives were treated like slaves'.

This was the final straw for the proud Iceni, who, led by Boudicca, made common cause with the Trinovantes, already keen to regain control of Colchester. In an orgy of destruction in AD 60 or 61, they paid back Rome for the insults they had been obliged to suffer for almost two decades.

Approaching Colchester, the rebels would have been pleased to discover that the settlement had neglected to construct walls and ditches, and the main fighting force available comprised retired soldiers. After two days of desperate defending, the Romans in Colchester retreated to the Temple of Claudius, confident that here at least they would be safe. They were mistaken, and the massacre which followed shocked even those familiar with such cruelty.

The present Norman castle is built on the platform of the Temple of Claudius and, even today, a tour through the castle dungeons is an unnerving experience, for they include the foundations of the Roman temple. It is the place where the final moments of Roman Colchester were extinguished. There are still buildings in Colchester's High Street where excavation has revealed a clear band of burnt soil that shows how total the colonia's destruction must have been.

Boudicca's next step was to destroy the strategic port of London. Then the army moved north to the town of Verulamium (St Albans), which they also sacked. Along the route of their advance, nothing survived. The Roman historian Tacitus speaks of 70,000 casualties: 'For the British did not take or sell prisoners, or practise other war-time exchanges. They could not wait to cut throats, hang, burn, and crucify.'

The Governor, Suetonius Paulinus, was an experienced general, and, somewhere in the Midlands, his men waited in their ranks to confront the enemy. That day, according to Tacitus, the Britons lost 80,000 and

THE NORMAN CASTLE AT COLCHESTER STANDS ON THE BASE OF THE TEMPLE
BUILT BY CLAUDIUS AND DESTROYED BY BOUDICCA.

the Romans a mere 400 dead. But the killing and suffering did not end
there. Unusually, such was the danger, the Roman army did not go into
winter quarters but campaigned throughout that winter, wiping out the
last pockets of resistance, and enslaving thousands of native Britons. A
terrible famine followed, for the harvests had been neglected.

Throughout East Anglia there is evidence to be seen of the horror and
destruction which took place during this dramatic year. Historians believe
an important result of the Iceni revolt for East Anglia was that it became
the property of the Emperor. It would explain the developments which
took place, particularly in the region of the Fens, which were drained
at this time. The Roman army had gone from defeat to victory and the
landscape tells a small part of the story.

In 1907 a boy fishing in the river Alde where it passes through the Suffolk
village of Rendham was astonished to find he had hooked up a full-size
bronze head! Following examination by the experts at the British Museum
it was thought likely to have been booty from the time of the Iceni revolt. It
had been hacked from a life-size statue of Claudius which had once stood
before the Temple of Claudius in Colchester. The jagged cuts about the neck

give an idea of the ferocity of the attack. There were probably enamel or glass beads in the eye sockets but they had long since been lost.

It is easy to imagine an Iceni warrior, proud of his part in the sacking of the hated Roman temple, making his way home carrying evidence of his prowess, but, pursued by an avenging Roman force, pausing at the Alde river crossing and reluctantly seeing the sense of parting company with such a dangerous trophy! In a moment it would have sunk beneath the water, and the action may have saved the warrior's life. Or, some people think it may have been cast into the water as a Celtic votive offering. That is very possible, as the Celts regarded the gods who dwelt in rivers and streams as allies to be acknowledged.

In Colchester Castle Museum there are displayed two Roman tombstones. One is of Marcus Favonius Facilis, a retired centurion of the XX legion, who had been part of the invasion army of AD 43 and died some time before the Boudiccan rebellion. He is depicted in full uniform, with a fine breastplate and a

TOMBSTONE OF MARCUS FAVONIUS FACILIS, FORMER CENTURION OF THE TWENTIETH LEGION. HE WAS PART OF THE ARMY WHICH INVADED BRITAIN IN AD 43. *(Colchester Castle Museum)*

magnificent decorated belt. He wears greaves to protect his legs in battle. He is armed with a sword and dagger, and the detail allows us to see how the equipment came together. He is holding a vine stick, the symbol of office for a centurion. Originally, the relief of Facilis would have been brightly painted in life-like colours. Beside his gravestone, which was found in 1868, was a lead cremation urn containing his ashes. Close by were pottery and glass containers holding the food and drink to accompany him on his final journey.

A similar scenario applies to the grave stone of Longinus Sdapeze. He was a junior cavalry officer in an auxiliary regiment of Thracians. Originally he came from Sofia, in present day Bulgaria. He is thought to have died at the age of 40, between AD 43 and 49, after 15 years' service. His figure once would have carried a spear in his right hand, which is formed to hold it, but that has long since vanished. He wears a leather tunic with shaped metal plates for added protection. He is depicted on his horse, riding over a native tribesman, who cowers in terror and seems to be naked. Oddly enough, the sack of Colchester by Boudicca may have enabled both these monuments to survive, because after the smoke cleared they were left face down in the ground, and so went ignored for well over a thousand years!

These are snapshots of momentous events and they are to be found in the soil all over East Anglia. Jordan Nye, a university student, was searching a field at Holbrook on the Suffolk coast in August 2004. When he found some well preserved metal objects he immediately informed the Portable Antiquities Scheme, as he was required to do, and next day archaeologists came to search for more. Soon they had uncovered a total of 30 metal objects, which, taken together with a few surviving pieces of leather, were found to comprise a complete set of Roman cavalry decorations of the sort we see in the tombstone of Longinus Sdapeze in Colchester Castle Museum. They had once adorned the mount of a Roman cavalry officer and there is every likelihood that they had been stolen as trophies from Colchester, and then, as the implications of defeat sank in, they were buried.

A similar story may well explain a discovery at Field Baulk, near March in Cambridgeshire and close to the Iceni hill-fort at Stonea. In 1982 a farmer, Samuel Hills, was digging his orchard to plant more apple trees. In the side of a drainage ditch he unearthed a clay pot containing

TOMBSTONE OF LONGINUS SDAPEZE, A
FORMER CAVALRY OFFICER WHO CAME TO
BRITAIN FROM HIS BIRTHPLACE IN BULGARIA.
(*Colchester Castle Museum*)

40 green-coloured objects, which he showed to his nephew Clive that evening. Next day the pair dug up the trees (!) and found 800 more coins.

A telephone call to the British Museum brought Dr Tim Potter, an ex-March Grammar School pupil and noted expert, who declared them to be silver coins of the Iceni tribe, and 'the largest such discovery ever made'. In total there were 872. Two of the coins had 'Ecen' and 'Ece' inscribed on them: only after the Roman invasion were coins so marked. The hoard was dated to about AD 60. Once again, the supposition is that these were buried in the aftermath of Boudicca's failed revolt. The coroner pronounced them to be treasure trove, and Mr Hills received compensation. A value of £100,000 was placed on the coins, which can be seen in the British Museum, still tumbling from the broken pot. March Museum has a dozen on display to whet the appetite!

THE CROWNTHORPE HOARD MAY ONCE HAVE BELONGED TO AN ICENI
LEADER WHO EMBRACED THE LIFE-STYLE OF HIS ROMAN CONQUERORS.
(*Norwich Castle Museum*)

In Norwich Castle Museum is yet another piece of evidence from this
period. The Crownthorpe Hoard is thought to have belonged to an Iceni
leader who also embraced the life-style of Rome. Here are seven items which
make up a drinking set, consisting of cups, bowls and saucepan-like warming
pans. They are all very Roman and indicate a villa life-style. Obviously they
belonged to someone who moved easily between the old and the new.

Another hoard was uncovered at Hockwold near Thetford. In 1962 Frank Curtis was walking through a wood, when he came across some badly damaged Roman silver drinking cups. They showed extremely high quality craftsmanship, and are objects of great beauty. They may once have graced the table of an important Roman official in Colchester or St Albans before they were carried off by a jubilant Iceni warrior. When the mood changed they would have lost their appeal. It is likely that they were crushed before being buried, so once again there is the prospect of them being associated with the hateful Roman conquerors and deliberately singled out for violent treatment. What happened to the owner? To be found in possession of such obvious loot would have invited a death sentence, or at least a life in shackles as a slave. The Hockwold cups as displayed by the British Museum have, of course, been restored.

Led by the new Procurator, Julius Classicianus, Britannia recovered remarkably quickly and the process of Romanisation continued. In particular, East Anglia became a rich region, its towns and cities connected by fine roads. The horrors of the rebellion might never have taken place.

In spite of its prosperity, East Anglia does not seem to have produced villa estates of the wealth we associate with the south and west of the country. At Stonea, where an Iceni rebellion had been crushed in AD 47, the evidence suggests that the grand building constructed outside the hill fort in the reign of Hadrian (the AD 130s), was more of an administrative centre – the estate headquarters – rather than an individual's property. It stood four storeys high, was 16 metres square, and had a hypocaust heating system, glass windows and fine mosaic floors. It may have been the headquarters for the Fen drainage project. The building lasted for just 50 years and the reason for its demolition has never been discovered or explained. The estate continued until the very end of the 4th century.

THE GRASS-COVERED RAMPARTS OF STONEA HILLFORT NEAR MARCH IN CAMBRIDGESHIRE. TACITUS GIVES AN ACCOUNT OF A BATTLE AGAINST THE ICENI THAT WAS FOUGHT HERE.

Of course, not all discoveries of coins have to be explained by conquest or rebellion. Some provide no clues as to their origin. At Howe in South Norfolk a metal detectorist, Christopher Pears, found a coin in a field near Sheep Lane in 1979. Soon after, more were uncovered, and by 1987 a total of 15 Roman gold aurei and 125 silver coins had been found. The latest possible date for the hoard is AD 87. There are no known historical events which could explain why they were abandoned.

After the defeat of Boudicca, Colchester was rebuilt and became the foremost town of East Anglia. The Trinovantes had a settlement about three miles south of the present town. Today, the native site is called Gosbecks, and a number of interesting finds have been made there which point to the importance of the area.

At Gosbecks, in about AD 150, the Romans built a temple dedicated to the god Mercury. This building stood in an enclosure of perhaps 91 square metres and the central room measured 7.6 metres square. The whole structure was surrounded by a veranda. There is a possibility that there was a tree or grove in the enclosure, which was the focal point of worship. Some experts think the temple may have served both Celtic and Roman gods, which would indicate the process of integration had been successful.

In 1945 Bert Beales was ploughing a field at Gosbecks Farm and turned up a bronze figurine. Not realising that it was Roman and very important, he took it home and put it in his garden shed. Two years later, quite by chance, it was brought to the attention of experts, who declared it to be the finest bronze statuette ever found in Great Britain. It depicts the Roman god Mercury, almost in the action of alighting on earth. It shows no influence of the Celtic craftsman, so may well be entirely classical in

THE BRONZE STATUETTE OF THE ROMAN GOD MERCURY FOUND AT GOSBECKS FARM. (*Colchester Castle Museum*)

inspiration. The present day Mercury Theatre in Colchester reminds us how famous the find was.

Religion in Roman times was able to embrace many of the old Celtic beliefs, for the conquerors only required loyalty to the Emperor, and once that was assured, the rest was a matter to be left alone. One aspect of Roman religion that confronts the archaeologist is the curse. If you were the victim of some sort of crime or injustice it was perfectly normal for you to write out the nature of your suffering, add some awful consequence for the perpetrator, and then leave it at the temple or sacred place. In 1889 at Fenhouse Farm, near Brandon in Suffolk, we have just such a tale of misfortune and anger. Coins were dredged from the river Little Ouse and with them was a bronze plaque reading: 'To the person slave or free who stole my pot, may they be cursed in the name of the god Neptune.' No doubt the words were shouted into the air and then the payment and message were thrown far out into the river. The evidence is now on display in Moyses Hall Museum, Bury St Edmunds.

The only Roman circus to be found in Britain was discovered outside Colchester in 2002. While not able to offer entertainment to provincials on the scale of Hollywood's *Ben Hur*, it would nevertheless have been spectacular, allowing as many as 8,000 peo-

THE COLCHESTER VASE WAS DISCOVERED IN 1848 AND THIS SIDE SHOWS NAMED GLADIATORS FIGHTING. (*Colchester Castle Museum*)

ple to support their chariot team. A little further outside the town, the site of the largest theatre in the province has been identified. Before 5,000 people, there would have been held gladiatorial contests as well as plays. At Hawkedon in south Suffolk a gladiator's helmet was found in 1965. Made of bronze, and twice as heavy as a standard legionary helmet, it would once have shone like silver, and earned appreciative cheers for its wearer.

But this theatre was dismantled just 50 years later, sometime after AD 200. It was not only closed, but the very building materials were removed. Colchester now had formidable walls encircling it, which stretched over 3,000 metres. Perhaps the countryside was no longer under firm Roman control. The age of the Anglo-Saxon raiders was dawning. In such a period of insecurity it would be natural to find evidence of people burying their goods in the ground for safety – and so we do.

Oliver's Orchard on the Gosbecks site was cleared of trees in May 1983, and the farmer uncovered a pot containing over 4,000 Roman coins. Close by was another pot, this time with 1,558 coins, and yet another was found with an additional 496. The finds in the orchard totalled 6,115 coins, and the latest date for burial of all the pots was AD 274. It is conjectured that they had been buried by the same individual within five years of each other. Of interest to coin experts was the fact that when they came to study the hoard, its value was lower than expected because the silver coins were found to contain copper in large quantities, an indication of difficult financial times. Only 1,600 had sufficient silver content to qualify as treasure trove. Some of the coins can be seen in the Colchester Castle Museum.

East of Ely is Prickwillow in Cambridgeshire. In the 1930s a beautiful skillet, or shallow saucepan, was found which provides evidence of how skilful Roman craftsmen could be in the 2nd century. It was made of bronze, with intricate detail on almost every surface. The handle is inlaid with worked foliage, including enamel. Around the bowl itself are dolphins, shells and sea serpents, swirling with weightless delight. The maker was sufficiently proud of his work to sign it with his name: Buduogenus. It offers further proof that the Fenland was a prosperous part of Roman Britain.

Returning to Colchester, there is another discovery which indicates that the town was enjoying a period of importance and success. The Colchester

Vase was found at West Lodge in 1848 and was in a remarkable state of preservation. Probably made there in about AD 175, it demonstrates the exquisite workmanship available to the rich and influential citizens. The vase is hailed as one of the finest pieces of ceramic art from the time of Roman Britain. It shows a hunting scene, and four gladiators fighting, a reminder of the popularity of such contests in the *colonia*. Above the fighters are their names: Secundus, Mario, Memnon and Valentius.

One of the attractions of treasure stories is that they are not always easy to corroborate. Tony Framlingham was a fisherman in Norfolk and one day in 1974 he caught some cod. He cut the fish open, intending to use it for bait, but there inside was a Roman coin! The coastline is constantly being eroded, and there have always been shipwrecks, but that still does not explain how the coin got into the fish. In a way it does not matter how the fish swallowed the coin – it's a great story. And here's another.

The village of Wingfield in Suffolk is dominated by a picturesque moated castle which dates from the Middle Ages. In 1836 a woman living close by had a dream which would change her life. She saw a finely dressed lady walking down a road she recognized – it was her own and it went right past her cottage. Just as the figure reached the pigsty in the garden, the woman vanished. Shocked that the dream was so vivid, the woman told her husband all about it and sent him with a spade to dig in the pigsty, which was at the bottom of their garden. He had hardly begun to dig before he found a great hoard of silver coins and other objects, which greatly amazed him.

Soon after, two strangers appeared at their cottage door and asked to see the treasure, which had become common knowledge in the village. The men offered to have it valued and promised to return with the profits. Foolishly, the couple gave them the silver cups and dishes and watched them leave the village, anticipating the fortune that would soon be theirs. Of course, they never saw the men, or their silver, ever again. But they had not handed over the coins, which were found to be Roman, and of enormous value, so they sold them and with the money they bought land on which they built a fine house. We may be sure that they lived happily ever after.

THE MILDENHALL
TREASURE

In a way, it all began in 1942, when farmer Fred Rolfe needed to deep plough his field at Thistley Green, Mildenhall, in Suffolk. He was planning to sow sugar beet, and that meant a twelve-inch furrow. However, he did not want to do the job himself, and that is how Gordon Butcher came to be there in his tractor, one freezing cold January afternoon, in a snowstorm, struggling to haul the plough across the field.

Suddenly, there was a jolt, and the engine roared. The plough had separated from the tractor. It was not unexpected, but given the appalling conditions it was most unwelcome. Butcher dismounted and prepared to excavate the problem, probably a tree root, which he knew would take some time. He knelt and scraped away the soil, creating a shallow pit, as he searched for the cause of the damage. He stopped when he felt a metal object, and then cleared around it. Suspecting it was of considerable size, and therefore that it would take time to move – and the snow was falling all the time – he decided he would enlist the help of Syd Ford, who lived close by. He knew that Ford collected objects thrown up by the plough, and sold them, so he would be the ideal person to assist him.

Ford worked as an agricultural engineer in West Row, and when Butcher told him about the buried metal object he needed no encouragement. Soon the two men were enlarging the hole, which was already two feet deep, and struggling to release something Ford would later describe as a round tray. At last it was beside them on the ground, already flecked with snow flakes. And then they found another tray, and then another, and so on. By the end of the afternoon, 34 articles were laid out on the snow-clad earth and the two men were exhausted and frozen stiff.

Ford took charge, suspecting that Butcher had no idea what they had found and was far more concerned to get home into the warm. The objects were all shapes and sizes and were caked in black corrosion. Ford put them all in his sack and announced he would take charge of them. He may well have told Butcher that they were pewter. Butcher by this time simply did not care!

For the next four and a half years Ford had the pieces to himself, and he fell in love with them, as only an avid collector can. He would later say: 'When I unearthed them they were black and very dirty, covered with quite a thick crust, which was very hard. You could not see a figure anywhere on them. It took me nearly two years to clean the

Sydney Ford could not bring himself to part with the Mildenhall treasure, and hid it away from public view.

big tray. I cleaned them with water, by continual washing.' Thrilled beyond belief with the products of his hard work, he placed them on his sideboard and only removed them when visitors called!

Ford clearly intended to keep all the objects for himself. He would have done so, too, had not events conspired to disclose his secret. Dr Hugh Fawcett was a fellow collector of interesting old things and was known to Ford from several visits he had made during the war. They both bought and sold historical artefacts. In June 1946 Dr Fawcett paid an unexpected visit to Ford, and during the course of their conversation words were said which would come to be regretted. Perhaps Ford was bursting with a desire to show off, or just wanted to share his pleasure, but he asked: 'Would you like to see some Roman pewter?'

Fawcett was taken into another room, and there on the sideboard he saw

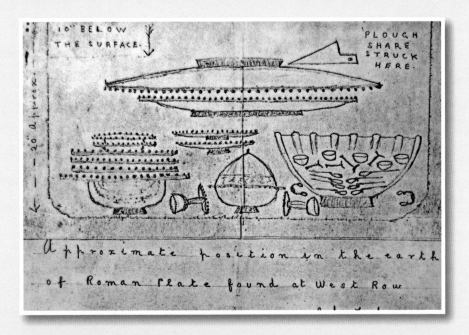

Within the drawing: 10" BELOW THE SURFACE. — 20" approx. — PLOUGH SHARE STRUCK HERE. — *Approximate position in the earth of Roman Plate found at West Row*

SYD FORD DREW A PLAN OF HOW THE MILDENHALL TREASURE WAS PLACED IN THE GROUND, AND HE EVEN INDICATED WHERE THE PLOUGH-SHARE STRUCK THE GREAT DISH.

two big dishes and a small bowl with some spoons in it. Now they were all clean and bright. The doctor was astonished: 'I immediately realized I was seeing something of immense and outstanding importance from the archaeological and national point of view.' Ford proceeded to open the sideboard and the full hoard was at last seen by his visitor.

Did Ford really believe they were pewter? It seems unlikely, as he was an experienced collector. But perhaps he had convinced himself that they were, knowing the consequences if they were silver. Alas for him, Dr Fawcett recognized exactly what they were, and insisted that Ford report them to the police without further delay, adding that if he did not, he would do so himself. That evening, after Dr Fawcett had departed, Ford must have understood how completely his private world had shattered. He spent his last few hours with a treasure which would be described as the richest and most beautiful ever found in Britain.

A few days later he received a letter from Dr Fawcett informing him of the correct steps he must take to inform the authorities. It is impossible not to feel sympathy for Ford that day, 21st June, as he entered Mildenhall police station and handed over 34 items of priceless silver to Sgt Cole, who gave him in return a receipt which looks like a laundry list and ends with the simple statement: 'Receipt given by Sgt Owen Cole when he confiscated the treasure from Syd Ford.'

The coroner, Mr Thomas Wilson, presided over the Treasure Trove inquest at Bury St Edmunds on Thursday, 1st July. Ford was required to explain how he came to be in possession of the articles, and predictably he maintained that he thought they were pewter. He claimed silver had not been found in the area before, whereas pewter was not particularly unusual. It was only after Dr Fawcett's visit earlier in the year that he understood exactly what it was he had been concealing. When asked what he had intended to do with them he replied, with disarming honesty: 'I did not intend to do anything with them – keep them. I was very proud of them.'

Gordon Butcher's evidence was brief and transparently honest. He claimed that Ford told him they were pewter, and he believed him. It is easy to imagine that during all the years when Ford was cleaning his silver, and then basking in the secret pleasure it gave him, the ploughman had not thought of it once!

GORDON BUTCHER, TRACTOR DRIVER AND THE FINDER OF THE MILDENHALL TREASURE, SHOWN HERE ON HIS WEDDING DAY – NOTE THE WHITE CARNATION!

The jury reached a predictable conclusion, which was that the articles found at Mildenhall were treasure trove, and so belonged to the Crown. In a sentence redolent of medieval grandeur, the coroner announced that, as a result, he 'now seized the silver as treasure trove in the name of the King'.

Only then did Butcher appreciate the

enormity of his misfortune. Had he announced the discovery of the treasure within days of finding it in the field in 1942, he would have been awarded a fortune – millions in today's money. But unfortunately for him, he allowed Ford to take it, and said nothing more. Because they had delayed until 1946 the court only gave them £1,000 each, a sum Butcher was delighted to accept.

Rolfe, the owner of the land, was having his hair cut in Bury St Edmunds, when another customer showed him a local newspaper, and he learnt of the fortune found on his land. Relations between Rolfe and Ford were said to be strained from that moment! According to the law of treasure trove in force at the time, Rolfe was not entitled to a share anyway, but it still hurt.

In 1977 Roald Dahl wrote a marvellous account of the finding of the Mildenhall Treasure, and it is no exaggeration to claim that for the majority of people it is the only version they know. But Dahl was not writing a historical narrative, he was a fiction writer, and it shows. His view of Ford is of a crafty, avaricious conman, who deceives the näive Butcher. Significantly, Ford had refused Dahl any assistance, and that may have coloured the writer's impression. But people in the Mildenhall area have taken exception to this portrait. They have a memory of a much gentler man, who genuinely collected items of historical value, loved them and on his death bequeathed them to the town museum, where they can be seen to this day.

The discovery made at Mildenhall has been described as 'one of the most important treasures of Roman silver ever found in the Roman Empire'. They are among the finest exhibits in the British Museum and are admired by visitors and scholars from around the world. Most of the pieces are believed to have been made in the Mediterranean region.

First out of the ground, and impossible to ignore, is the great dish, with a diameter of 60 cms. It has a rim made up of large beads, which helps to date it as 4th century. The outer rim of images shows a Bacchanalian revel, with lots of drink flowing freely, and a naked Bacchus (the god of wine) taking his leave. Hercules is so drunk he has to be supported by two satyrs. In the centre of the dish is the face of a magnificent sea god, which may be Neptune or Oceanus. He has a beard of seaweed and there are four dolphins in his hair. As a central feature of a villa entertainment it would have set the mood exactly!

Treasure Hoards in East Anglia

Two platters continued the Bacchic theme, indeed they were probably made in the same workshop, perhaps by the same person. One shows Pan with his pan pipes, known as syrinx, and he is facing a maenad, who plays a double flute. The other platter shows a dancing satyr and another maenad. They are surrounded by symbolic creatures and objects. What makes these two platters especially interesting is that on the back of both is the scratched name 'Eutherios', as though they were a personal gift to someone.

There are six flanged bowls of varying sizes, and they also have the large bead rim. They have outer rims depicting animals like bulls, bears, leopards, sheep and griffins. One of the centre medallions shows the head of a young woman, while another has an armed head which may be Alexander the Great. His mother Olympias could be the lady with the covered head depicted in another bowl.

The large covered bowl offers an unexpected detail, because its lid, which is decorated with a frieze of profile heads and mythical animals, was made almost a century earlier, judging by its style, and does not even fit. It was presumably made in the 3rd century for another bowl, now lost. The handle is formed from a figure blowing a conch shell.

Two goblets are, at first glance, rather unusual, for they appear to have bases which are too big for them. But they are designed for a dual purpose, as the user could turn them upside down, to find that the base is a decorated platter – clever and functional, the dream of all designers! Five ladle bowls, of which four have handles in the form of dolphins, are also among the hoard.

THE MILDENHALL TREASURE – THE RICHEST AND MOST BEAUTIFUL
TREASURE EVER FOUND IN BRITAIN. (*British Museum*)

And finally there are eight spoons, in various styles, but all with pear-shaped bowls. Two of them are particularly important to the collection as a whole because they are inscribed 'Pascentia Vivas' and 'Papittedo Vivas' – 'Long life to Pascentia/Papittedo'. It is exciting when the names of two people sound across almost 2,000 years, and are recorded on objects they would have touched and valued. Three spoons have the Christian Chi-Rho monogram between the symbols of alpha and omega. While most of the silverware is hardly Christian, the discovery that some must be has contributed to the identification of Flavius Lupicinus – a man of wealth and power and the commander of the Roman armies in the West – as the possible owner. Caught up in a fight for the Imperial throne, he had left Britain in AD 360, never to return.

The lack of documented evidence about the Mildenhall discovery has led to all sorts of strange theories about how it came to be in the ground. For a time it was thought it may have been brought into England from somewhere in southern Europe by an American airman flying into the base at Mildenhall. It would have been recovered and sold after the war goes the theory, except Ford and Butcher found it first. This is most unlikely, and even more so when it is realized Mildenhall was not a USAF base at the time.

Another regular legend concerns the 'missing pieces'. What if Ford held on to two items and sold them later? Proponents of this idea believe they can see items in the background of Ford's photograph which did not form part of the declared treasure. Once again, it is unlikely, and, knowing what we do about Ford and his genuine love of the collection, it is difficult to imagine he would have sold any bits he had managed to retain.

But of all the alternative versions of the truth, pride of place must go to the Seaber family, whose story triumphs on the grounds of sheer complexity. The central point of their saga is that the Roman treasure was found almost a century earlier and had been reburied.

In 1809 the land where the treasure would one day be found belonged to Gage Farm. In that year John 'Black Jack' Seaber married Sarah, the farmer's daughter, and in time took over the farm. They produced a family of four sons and two daughters. When his wife Sarah died, in 1850, 'Black Jack' handed the running of the farm to his eldest son, William, and moved about a mile away. Black Jack remarried, and when he died in 1867 he left everything, including the farm, to this second wife, Mary Ann, and absolutely nothing to his children. If William Seaber had found treasure on Gage Farm land he

MILDENHALL MUSEUM IS THE PERFECT PLACE TO START ANY EXPLORATION OF THE STORY. IT HAS AN EXCELLENT DISPLAY AND THE ATTENDANTS ARE HELPFUL AND KNOWLEDGEABLE.

was not about to give it to his stepmother Mary Ann, preferring to hide it instead.

Mary Ann died in 1907, and the farm passed out of the Seaber family's ownership. In 1923, so the story goes, descendants of the Seaber family attempted to take possession of their buried treasure, but because a stile on the old footpath had been relocated, all their measurements proved to be futile. An archaeologist, Thomas Lethbridge, excavated a small Roman villa at nearby Thistley Green in the 1930s, and while doing so he uncovered an old Victorian trunk in a pit. Had it once held the Seaber treasure?

There are so many things we do not know about the Mildenhall Treasure, and it can be frustrating, but stand in front of the cabinet in the British Museum, wonder at the skill of unknown Roman silversmiths, and it all becomes irrelevant.

THE THETFORD TREASURE

The first Christian missionaries may have arrived in the second half of the 2nd century AD and from this period comes the story of the first martyr, St Alban, who died rather than give up his newly-acquired beliefs. But it would be wrong to assume that late Roman Britain was Christian, far from it. The Celtic and Roman gods continued to dominate the lives of the majority of the people. To the very end of the Roman era, Britain was a predominantly pagan land and, apparently, quite content to be so! Religion to the Romans was a delightful 'pick and mix' and they liked it that way.

'In 1844 some labourers, when carting sand from a hill near the Hall, found two beautiful Roman urns containing a variety of brazen figures and ornaments' – White's *1845 Norfolk Directory* is rather lacking in detail, but the objects survive in the British Museum and give an interesting insight into religious beliefs in the middle of the Roman period of occupation. They were found at Felmingham Hall and may once have formed part of the rituals in a shrine or temple. Significantly, they combine Celtic and Roman deities. There are fine heads of Jupiter and Minerva, but also a pair of ravens which may suggest continuity with earlier customs. Even more fascinating is the presence of a wheel, which might refer to a curious blend of pagan and Christian belief, with its implication of resurrection, as the wheel in myth was set alight and rolled into a river, whereupon it rose and was recreated as a god of the sky.

Arthur and Greta Brooks were driving through Thetford, returning home to Norwich, one grey November evening in 1979, when Mrs Brooks noticed a large building site, complete with excavators, lorries and the usual tangles of wires and posts – but no people. This was Gallows

Norfolk hoard of Roman gold

Roman gold treasures, described by the British Museum as being very important both historically, and archaeologically, have been found at Thetford.

Among the hoard, which consists of 77 objects in gold and silver, as well as some beads, are 33 silver spoons, which bear an important collection of religious

Dr. Tim Potter, assistant keeper in charge of Romano-British collections at the British Museum, said that most of the pieces were characteristic in style of the fourth and early fifth centuries AD, suggesting that they may have been buried around 410 AD when the

been completed, Potter. "It is a very discovery archaeolog historically. It is o the greatest value to Mr. Tony Gre officer with the Archaeological

THE SAD QUESTION IS NOT "WHAT WAS FOUND HERE?" BUT WHAT IS LOST
FOR GOOD BENEATH THE CONCRETE.

Hill, soon to become the Fison Way Industrial Estate. Arthur Brooks had been the proud owner of a metal detector for two years, and enjoyed making expeditions when it could be put to work. Greta suggested to her husband that he should check over the site for a few minutes with the metal detector. He was reluctant to stop, no doubt aware that the odds of him finding anything were slight. He probably also reflected that he had no right to be there. But he started to walk across a patch of ground which all too clearly bore the marks of massive disturbance.

It was getting dark when he heard the first signal. Kneeling, he scraped away the earth and came upon some spiked items, which would later be identified as spoon handles. Soon he had uncovered a shale box and more and more items took their place beside him. His astonishment can only be imagined. He must have known that what he was doing was illegal, and he was about to make it worse. He wrapped all the items in his anorak, bundled it into the car and then he and his wife drove home to Norwich. Did they talk throughout the journey or were they silent?

On arrival he washed the items, doubtless stared at them in disbelief and then packed them away. What he did with them over the next six months

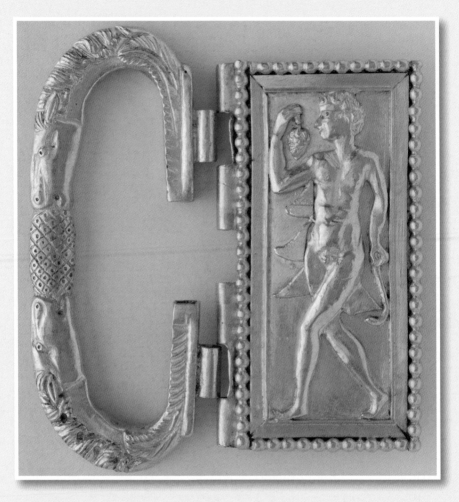

THE GOLD BUCKLE FROM THE THETFORD HOARD MAY HAVE BEEN A VOTIVE
OFFERING FROM A ROMAN SOLDIER. THE SATYR CONNECTS IT TO THE CULT
OF BACCHUS. (*British Museum*)

is lost to us, but he must have known he had found gold, and so he surely
knew that he was obliged to declare his find to the police. Perhaps he did
feel uneasy and mention it to others – or maybe his wife did.

Soon the existence of some sort of spectacular treasure came to the ears of Tony Gregory of the Norfolk Archaeological Service, and he eventually tracked down the Brooks. In May 1980 he called at their College Road house. He was taken to a bank vault (further proof that Arthur Brooks knew exactly what he had found) and presumably experienced that rare moment in an archaeologist's life – professional surprise and delight. But his excitement would have been tempered by one depressing realisation: the six-month delay meant there was no chance of excavating the Gallows Hill site, which now had a warehouse built on top of it. In all probability other, equally wonderful, objects were effectively lost forever.

Arthur Brooks was suffering from terminal cancer throughout this time, and so it was not easy to point the finger at him and accuse him of anything more than folly. In strictly legal terms the Brooks were guilty of trespass and so the coroner's inquest in 1981 had to take this into account when it declared the Thetford Treasure to be the property of the Crown. Mrs Brooks was never going to receive the full monetary value because of the delay in announcing the discovery. Mr Brooks had died meanwhile – indeed, her defence made the point that owing to his medical condition Arthur Brooks had other things on his mind than visiting a police station! As it was, the Diss District Coroner, Mr Ernest Clarke, directed that Mrs Greta Brooks should share part of the £261,540 he awarded to Breckland District Council. The Treasury were far from keen to pay up in these circumstances, and it was the intervention of a Treasury minister, reminding them of the emotional factors, that made them eventually provide the money.

Once the hoard was in the care of the British Museum it was possible to clean it properly and assess its importance. Dr Timothy Potter enthused: 'The hoard should be ranked with the very great treasures of Roman Britain, with those from Mildenhall and Water Newton.' Richard Hobbs, Curator at the British Museum said: 'The Thetford Treasure is of national and international importance, as it contains one of the finest sets of late Roman silver plate and jewellery known from the late Roman period.' In total the whole treasure includes 44 pieces of jewellery, 33 silver spoons, three strainers and a shale box. What was it doing there?

The site may itself be a clue. In the Iron Age, Gallows Hill had been the location of a hill fort, with three great ditches enclosing a number of large timber buildings. There may even have been an avenue of sacred oak trees. It is thought that it was a religious centre for the Iceni, as it overlooks the river Little Ouse, and is on the route of the Icknield Way, one of the oldest trackways in Britain. Inevitably, the Boudiccan revolt brought destruction to the Iceni religious centre, but in time it rose again in the form of a Roman temple.

One of the first surprises when the jewellery was examined was the discovery that it was in near-perfect condition. Some of it had never been worn, indeed some pieces were unfinished. This suggested that the original owner was a jeweller, working in France or Britain in the final years of the Empire, perhaps AD 390. It is thought likely that the entire collection was created in the same workshop, perhaps by the same craftsman. The purity of the treasure is exceptional – the gold pieces range from 89% to 95% and the silver 90% to 99%.

The pagan nature of the hoard was unmistakeable. Of the 33 inscribed silver spoons, twelve bore inscriptions to Faunus, a minor pagan cult in Britain, indeed they were the first evidence that it had followers in this country. Faunus was a god who protected livestock and ensured success at harvest time. He was a nature god, like Pan, whose sacred sites were not necessarily to be found in temples, but in open woodland, in the countryside or by the side of a stream. A spoon inscription reads: 'Deiifauninari' or 'Faunus the Mighty'. The worship of gods like Faunus was threatened once the Empire embraced Christianity, and there were times when the old believers were the victims of persecution. At such times it is conceivable that the trappings of pagan worship would be buried, perhaps in a sacred place, in the hope that toleration would return and they could be reinstated.

Today, all the treasures are in the British Museum. One of the most splendid pieces is a gold belt buckle, displaying a satyr, another clue which suggests devotion to Bacchus, the god of wine. It may have been a votive offering from a Roman soldier. Of the 22 gold rings, all exquisitely crafted, with precious and semi-precious stones, there are more reminders of Faunus, for not only is there a horned head of the god himself, but there are woodpeckers, a bird connected with his cult. There are also bracelets, necklaces and pendants. The largest gold bracelet weighs over 100 grams.

Sixteen of the 33 inscribed spoons had swan's neck handles, while seventeen were larger, with long pointed handles. One shows Triton, a merman with a human body and a fish tail, with a dolphin, while another depicts a leaping tigress, and a third has the image of a fish. A few of the spoons bore signs of slight wear, which suggested that they may have been used in worship. Three perforated spoons could have been used to strain wine.

COINS FROM GOOD EASTER, NEAR CHELMSFORD, MAY WELL BE AMONG THE
LAST MINTED WHILE BRITAIN WAS PART OF THE ROMAN EMPIRE.
(*Chelmsford Museum*)

A year earlier, and close to the site, over 70 Roman silver coins were found. They are believed to be another hoard buried during times of trouble or danger sometime between AD 383 and 388. The obvious suggestion is that they too are connected with the sacred site.

Just a few miles from Thetford is Hockwold cum Wilton. In 2006 a metal detectorist discovered some items of metalwork which indicated the site of a temple complex that lasted to the late 4th century – the very end of Roman Britain. This would not have been unexpected, for the Fenland region was densely populated and intensely farmed throughout the Roman period and the old beliefs were never eradicated. The finds suggested offerings to the nature gods, who may have been Cybele, a fertility goddess, and her lover Attis. There is also a small naked figure of

THE ANCIENT HOUSE MUSEUM AT THETFORD CONTAINS MANY INTERESTING DISPLAYS OF LOCAL HISTORY, AND ON OCCASIONS HOLDS EXHIBITIONS OF NATIONAL TREASURES.

a horned god carrying a ritual trophy. Thetford Museum has a fine display of the discoveries.

Roman civilisation meant towns – fine stone forums, temples, baths and market places. Traditionally, the province basked in the security afforded by Hadrian's Wall, far to the north, but the new enemies were on all the Imperial frontiers and were preparing to cross the North Sea. The northern defences would become irrelevant.

In the middle of the 3rd century the coastline of East Anglia was attacked by boatloads of raiders who came from across the North Sea, and, in the 4th century, it is clear that Britain suffered a succession of invasions which almost overwhelmed the depleted forces available. It is this background which explains the many discoveries of treasure in the soil. What survive today are the hoards which were unclaimed, and the dramatic conclusion must be that the owners were no longer able to return. There must be many more still to be found – an exciting prospect for the metal detectorist!

In Roman times Chelmsford was known as Caesaromagus. In the excellent museum is a truly stunning collection of Roman gold coins known as *solidi*, which were found about six miles to the north-west at Good Easter. In their way they provide the perfect illustration of this period of decline. Chelmsford was abandoned by AD 400, probably unable to survive amid the lawlessness and shortages which accompanied the chaos all around it. The Good Easter coins were found by various people in the 1990s and apart from being objects of extraordinary perfection, all but one of the coins were minted in Italy between AD 394 and 406. So they are in a way, our last view of Roman Britain.

CHURCH SILVER AT WATER NEWTON

When, in February 1975, Alan Holmes set out to walk in the fields near Water Newton, Peterborough, he can have had no idea that he was about to find the oldest set of Christian church silver in the world.

Striding between the newly-ploughed furrows, he noticed something grey and interesting standing proud of the soil. He knew it was made of silver and knelt to examine it. He carefully removed what may once have been a tray and looked to see if there was more to be found. The ground was soon covered with 26 separate articles, all caked in soil and corrosion, but all clearly made of silver. He had made a discovery of international importance, which now may be viewed in the British Museum.

Water Newton had once been known as Durobrivae – 'the fort by the bridge', and had stood guard over one of the bridges along Ermine Street, the road to the north and the present-day A1. In time, a settlement grew up around it and, as the centuries passed and the dangers increased, ditches and walls were added, which offered substantial protection to the inhabitants of both fort and town.

Durobrivae has been described as one of the richest towns in Britain, and the source of the wealth was pottery, which was produced on what was almost a factory scale. A mortarium was discovered which was inscribed: 'Sennianus the potter of Durobrivae fired this'. If only all craftsmen had signed their work! Not surprisingly a few people became very rich and were able to build lavish villas for their families. One was so vast that for a long time archaeologists thought it was another town! Such a family, with their wealth and contacts, was likely to be aware of the new religion

THIS WAS ONCE THE SITE OF THE ROMAN TOWN OF DUROBRIVAE, BUILT
BESIDE THE ROMAN ROAD – NOW THE A1 – WHICH STILL CARRIES TRADE
NORTH AND SOUTH.

of Christianity, and to have invested in a personal collection of church silver, which either belonged to them or to the long-lost church itself.

When the silverware was examined it was found to have been made at different times and in different places, but it appeared to be essentially Christian in purpose and to have been buried in the very late 4th century. As the Church grew in strength it attracted hostility from other beliefs, and there were times when Christians were persecuted. Burying the church silver in the ground may have made sense at the time. Of course, it is possible that the owner was simply caught up in the general lawlessness caused by the periodic invasions and resulting disorder.

Nine of the articles were used during worship, such as a magnificent decorated wine carafe, a wine strainer, and several other items, all with a specific purpose. Of particular interest is a silver mixing bowl, which is inscribed to show it was a gift from a faithful Christian: 'I Publianus, honour your sacred shrine, trusting in you, O Lord'. These are all exquisite examples of the very finest craftsmanship, and they were dedicated to God in a clear statement of devotion. Most of the people in the area may have worshipped the old gods, but it looks as though the rich and powerful were embracing the new faith.

Christianity drew on many aspects of earlier, pagan beliefs, and one of these was the votive offering. The Water Newton hoard produced 18 silver plaques, which had been given to the church perhaps to accompany prayers, or to offer thanks for a received blessing. The Chi Rho symbol appears on nine of them, and three even have names on them – Amcilla, Innocentia, Viventia – which probably indicate gifts from individual members of the congregation. So few names of people have survived from the centuries of Roman Britain that it is remarkable one treasure hoard produced so many.

THE WATER NEWTON HOARD IS PROBABLY THE OLDEST SET OF CHRISTIAN CHURCH SILVER IN THE WORLD. (*British Museum*)

THE HOXNE HOARD

'The farmer asked me to find some tools which he had dropped and ploughed in.' With those words began one of British archaeology's greatest discoveries and, incidentally, a text-book example of what the professionals can achieve when everything goes right.

Peter Whatling was the tenant of Home Farm, Hoxne, and when he lost a hammer in a field he asked his friend Eric Lawes to search for it, knowing he would be glad of the excuse. Recently retired, on his birthday, Eric had been given a metal detector by his wife and so it was that on Monday, 16th November 1992, he began his search of the field.

When he found a coin, his excitement was kindled, for, as he explained: 'I have found badges, buttons and silver paper before, but nothing like this.' Soon he had another coin, and by now the signals from his detector were so loud he knew he was on to something exceptional. 'I probed down to the bottom of the ploughed soil and uncovered hundreds more Roman coins. There were so many I had to run to the farmhouse and ask the farmer to help me gather them all up.'

The two of them scooped out more coins, and when they had accumulated about a thousand they put them into a bag. Only at this moment did Eric Lawes realize he could be about to become a rich man!

What had happened so far was marvellous, but it was not that different from all the other treasure finds that make for good newspaper stories. All that was about to change, because farmer Peter Whatling did exactly what metal detectorists are supposed to do. He contacted Chris Storey, the assistant county land agent, because Home Farm was rented from Suffolk County Council. He in turn put in a call to the county archaeological department and to the coroner.

When Storey arrived on the scene he knew this was a moment he would never forget. 'I was quite flabbergasted by the quality of the find. The farmer had pulled out a gold chain with a circular pendant with precious stones in it. It looked like somebody's official regalia. Also two rings and a bag of spoons were found, and they were of exceptional quality. There was also a massive bag of coins, both gold and silver; thousands were found in total.'

But once they had called in the experts, they left the site as it was. When Judith Plouviez of the Suffolk Archaeological Unit arrived, she appreciated the action they had taken. Most unusually, her team would now be able to excavate the site properly, and in its entirety. As a result they discovered details that would normally have been lost forever. Throughout the night a police guard was placed on the site, and the next day, 17th November, the excavation was completed. Not only did they take out the mass of coins and other articles which were obviously of interest, but being experts in their field – and also, having the site in near-perfect condition – they were able to do much more. Every find·location was plotted and photographed.

HERE, IN A FIELD JUST OUTSIDE HOXNE, ERIC LAWES WENT IN SEARCH OF AN OLD HAMMER AND FOUND A TREASURE WHICH ASTONISHED THE EXPERTS.

By the end of an extraordinary day, the Hoxne hoard was secure in Halesworth police station, and the villagers knew that they had earned themselves an index entry in all subsequent books about late Roman Britain! As for the ploughed field, it was soon able to conceal its memories beneath swaying golden wheat, confident that the eternal cycle of the seasons would endow it with anonymity.

Rarely has archaeology appeared on the front page of the *Sun* newspaper, but it did on Thursday, 19th November under the banner headline: 'Bootyfull! Eric Finds £10m Booty'. The Hoxne hoard captured the public's imagination, not just because it was such a valuable discovery (although the *Sun* was guilty of some exaggeration) but because the participants were so obviously likeable and they had all done the right thing.

From the first it was clear the hoard was exceptional. Judith Plouviez left no room for doubt when interviewed: 'This hoard is one of the finest from Roman Britain. We found a disintegrated box full of valuable objects. At the bottom were two silver figurines, a human bust and a lioness with two small silver containers. There were also spoons, decorated strainers, gold bracelets and necklaces and thousands of coins. These provide the best dating evidence for the hoard and show it was hidden at the end of the Roman period, 1,600 years ago.'

Upon its arrival at the British Museum for study and conservation, a spokesman agreed, describing it as 'the most valuable find of Roman coins ever to have been recovered in Britain'. It was difficult to disagree as there were almost 15,000 of them, five times more than any previous discovery! There were about 200 other treasure objects. In mere terms of weight there were 3.5 kilograms of gold (7.72 lbs) and 25 kilograms of silver (55.1 lbs).

On 3rd September 1993 the coroner's inquest took place at Lowestoft. It reached the conclusion that the treasure had been deliberately hidden with the intention it should be recovered later. This led to a verdict of treasure trove and the hoard became the property of the Crown. The British Museum was now able to acquire it for the nation, but had to pay the full market value to the finder, and this sum would be determined by an independent committee. Two months later the Hoxne treasure was officially valued at £1.75m and by April of the next year the British Museum had raised the sum by way of various grants and donations. Eric Lawes became an extremely rich man. He immediately split this sum with farmer

THE HOXNE HOARD

WHAT MADE THE HOXNE HOARD SUCH A GOOD NEWSPAPER
STORY WAS NOT JUST THAT IT WAS BEAUTIFUL AND
VALUABLE, BUT THAT EVERYONE DID EXACTLY WHAT THEY
WERE SUPPOSED TO DO.

ROMAN FORTUNE FOUND IN FIELD

'I could be a rich man'

By Mark Hindle and Guy Campbell

RETIRED gardener Eric Lawes struck gold when he stumbled across one of the greatest hoards of Roman treasure ever found in Britain.

Experts say the spectacular haul of thousands of gold coins found by chance on a farm in north Suffolk could be worth millions.

Mr Lawes, 70, of Hoxne Road, Denham, was searching for old farm tools as a favour to a nearby farmer when he noticed a small silver coin on the ground.

Using a metal detector he found another coin and followed the trail until the signal grew louder. He uncovered the remains of a pot and saw a heap of gold coins.

"I took about a thousand coins and put them in a bag. I could be a rich man, I hope so," he said.

"The farmer asked me to find some tools which he had dropped and ploughed in. It was just by luck."

East Anglian Daily Times, Thursday, November 19, 1992

Peter Whatling, and then turned his attention to what he would do with his share. Initially he had wanted to move house and build a bigger one elsewhere, but his wife Greta was having none of that, saying, 'I don't want to move. I'm happy here.' So, they built themselves a new bungalow close by and remained in the village of Denham.

Only when the conservators at the British Museum began their work could they appreciate the extraordinary set of circumstances which had preserved the hoard in its context. The box measured 60 x 45 x 30 cm and the contents had obviously been packed with enormous care and skill. The presence of small silver padlocks indicated there had been smaller boxes within it, and that they had been leather-clad because fragments of the leather survived in place. Some of the more compact parts of the excavation had been taken to the laboratory as clumps of soil, and these were now separated and examined. Five silver bowls had been stacked in the box and the Roman owner had used hay to protect them from scratches and distortion. From the distribution of the coins it was clear that they had been in textile bags which had been eased into the gaps between the larger articles. The process of burial had been thought out in advance, and carried out with great care.

The chest of treasure was placed in the ground sometime between AD 420 and 450. It was in 410 that the Emperor Honorius famously wrote to the citizens of Britain, explaining that he could no longer offer them the protection of the Roman army, and adding that in future 'they must look to themselves'.

Museums usually display coins in orderly lines of gold and silver discs on a tasteful felt background, with individual labels, informing the viewer of the particular points of interest. It is obviously the sensible, scholarly way to present such things. But the display of the Hoxne hoard looks as though it came from a pirate movie, a cascade of fabulous wealth in its most tangible form. A mass of gold and silver assails the eye, jumbled into all sizes and hues. It is as though a person simply emptied a bag of them into the display cabinet. The wonderful sound of them tumbling on to the tray is easy to imagine!

There are 569 gold *solidus* coins, all in excellent condition, and showing an astonishing 99% level of purity. Eight Roman emperors are represented on them and, while the coins do not have dates, it is possible to bracket their manufacture between AD 365 and 404. The relatively short time span means few, if any, show signs of wear, which is usually a common problem with coins. The majority of the gold coins found were made during the reigns of the emperors Arcadius and Honorius. None of the hoard was minted in Britain, but came from Rome, Milan and Ravenna, the last named city being the residence of emperors at this time. The majority of the coins – 14,205 of them – were silver and here the range of emperors represented is wider – a total of 15, in fact. Most of the silver coins were minted in Germany, France and Italy.

The clipping of coins appears to be a very British habit, right down to relatively modern times, and is well represented in this collection. The coins had a purity of 90%, which made them very reliable as exchange, but this was reduced when a tiny v-shaped bit was cut out and kept. On its own a clipping is tiny, and not worth much, but take a thousand clippings, melt them down and you have a considerable asset – without any charge! Clever metal workers could forge new coins using the clippings, indeed the Hoxne hoard has a number as evidence. Obviously the practice was unlawful and carried serious penalties, but that did not prevent people doing it. There were also some bronze coins and the inferior forgeries!

Jewellery was well represented in the hoard, and all 29 pieces were of exceptional quality. There were six necklaces, some of which are finely plaited in gold, and they have animal heads at the clasp ends. Two of the three finger-rings were threaded onto the necklace chains, while the third was discovered among the mass of coins. All had once possessed precious stones but they had been taken out before the burial in the chest.

Small statues from Roman Egypt sometimes display a female figure wearing a body chain which crosses the chest and back, with ornate plaques where they cross. At Hoxne such a chain was found, where one of the plaques had spaces for nine gemstones, and the other still had a coin in the centre. The *solidus* coin date was towards the end of the 4th century, dating the reign of Gratian. It was clear the wearer had been very small or very young.

THE HOXNE HOARD SHOWS LATE ROMAN CRAFTSMANSHIP AT ITS BEST.
(British Museum)

There were 19 bracelets of the sort we would describe as bangles. Within the group are two sets of four, one of which provides interesting parallels with those found at nearby Thetford, in 1979. The largest bracelet was intended to be worn on the upper arm and displays the craftsman's skill by way of minute punched holes which form patterns known as pierced work, resembling lace. The best of the bracelets is also in pierced work, but it provides the name of the wearer. The inscription, worked around the entire band, says: 'Be happy with this, Lady Juliana'. This is particularly exciting because it means the bracelet was created for a named individual, who may have been known to the owner of the Hoxne hoard.

There were 78 spoons packed away in the chest, all carefully stacked and protected. Ten of them bear the name of an individual, Aurelius Ursicinus, and it is no tiny and hidden identity, but a proud statement, for it sits within the bowl of the spoons for all to read. For this reason it is thought likely that he was the owner of the treasure when it was buried, although, sadly, nothing else is yet known about him. On other spoons were the names Peregrinus, Faustinus and Silvicola. Who they were is unknown.

As mentioned earlier, by the end of Roman Britain Christianity was probably well established among the civil and military aristocracy. The Hoxne hoard provides evidence that the owner was a Christian and possibly used some of the silverware during whatever services were celebrated. Out of 20 long-handled silver ladles, with deep round bowls, ten have the familiar Chi-Rho insignia on them.

Among the more spectacular and unusual articles found was a solid cast silver statuette of a prancing tigress, which may once have formed the handle of a thin-necked vase, now lost. There were also four pepper pots, which are objects of great beauty and ingenuity. Pepper was an exotic spice from the Far East and only the richest members of society would have been familiar with it, let alone its silver-crafted dispensers. One of these shows a late Roman empress in a formal pose, with expertly dressed hair, and wearing a fine gown, complete with a jewelled necklace. Another shows Hercules wrestling a giant, while the remaining pair depict animals. Taken together, these items hint at a grace and magnificence slightly at odds with the conventional view of Britain in chaos, reeling beneath successive barbarian invasions.

An interesting insight into Roman toilet concerns was provided by the inclusion of nine implements which have been identified as toothpicks and ear-cleaners. The latter are beautifully worked in the graceful shape of an ibis. There were also three dolphin and leopard-handled objects, which may once have been cosmetic brushes. All these things belonged to a family able to enjoy the very highest standard of life.

The Hoxne hoard may be viewed today in the British Museum, where it delights and amazes the thousands who crowd the Roman galleries. There was a delightful human touch when the treasure was first displayed. While the public studied the coins, bracelets, necklaces and all the other items of gold and silver, they came upon a surprising object, much more familiar to them, which was nevertheless thought worthy of a place in the national collection. Reminding them of how Eric Lawes came to be in that field in the first place was the object of his original search – a grubby, well-used hammer.

Sutton Hoo

The Sandlings is the coastal area of Suffolk but, paradoxically, it may have been settled by invaders later than the rest of the county. The Wash provided easy access to the rich heartland of East Anglia, and the network of rivers, like the Ouse, Nene and Lark, meant that West Stow existed before Ipswich. But that was all about to change with the arrival of ships from Sweden.

Known as the Wuffings, after their leader, these people were related to the royal house of Sweden, and they brought with them traditions which are unique to that country, including the burial of their leaders in boat graves.

Rendlesham, beside the river Deben in Suffolk, appears to have been their tribal centre. In 1687 a gold crown is said to have been found there, but for all sorts of reasons that is unlikely – not least because crowns were not part of the royal regalia of that period! It was the Wuffings who created Ipswich as their trading port, the first known town in Britain since the Roman period.

Snape, to the west of Aldeburgh, was where they buried a great leader in about AD 550, and they buried him in a boat. The site was excavated in 1862 and, regrettably, much of the evidence has been lost. The boat was not large, perhaps 14 metres long, with a beam of 3 metres, but it evidently once held a grave. A fine gold ring with beaded filigree work and Roman intaglio was found, which may now be admired in the British Museum. At the time, the rusty iron bolts did not cause much excitement and ended up in the Aldeburgh Museum, but they were to play a key role in the story which follows.

The settlement at Rendlesham prospered and, by the end of the 6th century, the Wuffings controlled all of Norfolk and Suffolk. Perhaps it was at this time the Wuffing cemetery moved from Snape to a new site called Sutton Hoo. Woodbridge did not exist on the Deben's west bank at this time, so mariners on their way to the tribal centre would have seen only the mounds to former leaders on the high ground to the east, which impressively proclaimed the status of the man they were soon to meet.

By AD 600 the ambitious leader of these people was Raedwald and he led the East Angles to become the dominant power in southern England, recognized as such by other client kingdoms. In 604 Raedwald was baptized into the Christian faith by Augustine, in Kent, but when he returned to Rendlesham he was persuaded to return to his pagan creed. In 617 he was acclaimed as *Bretwalda*, the supreme warrior leader in England, and received the symbols of office – the standard and the whetstone. For a brief moment, East Anglia was the uncontested seat of English power.

When he died in AD 624 or 625, Raedwald's funeral must have been lavish and memorable. He had taken the kingdom to unprecedented heights, giving his people security and status. As they watched the boat carry his body from Rendlesham to Sutton Hoo, they must have known that dangerous times lay ahead for all of them. Raedwald had left his people in this world and they sent him on his way to the next.

Monday 8 May 1939. Arrived at Sutton Hoo and after leaving my luggage at Mr Lyon's house, where I lodged in 1938, interviewed Mrs Pretty, who accompanied me to the mounds. I asked which one she would like opened and she pointed to Mound 1, the largest barrow of the group, and said, 'What about this?'

With that entry in his diary Basil Brown embarked on what would become the greatest archaeological discovery in British history. Mrs Edith Pretty, a widow, lived at Sutton Hoo in

BASIL BROWN WAS SELF-TAUGHT BUT SHOWED HIMSELF TO BE A GENIUS AT THE BUSINESS OF ARCHAEOLOGICAL EXCAVATION.

DARK AGE SHIPS SAILING UP THE RIVER DEBEN TO THE ROYAL PALACE AT
RENDLESHAM WOULD HAVE PASSED THE BURIAL GROUND AT SUTTON HOO
(TO THE RIGHT, ABOVE THE FARM).

a grand white house overlooking the town of Woodbridge on the opposite
bank of the river Deben. Her late husband had never achieved his ambition
of excavating the fern-covered mounds which were clustered together
nearby, and now she was fulfilling his wishes. Basil Brown was an amateur
archaeologist, occasionally employed by Ipswich Museum, and he had
returned in the summer of 1939 to continue the work which so far had
been unspectacular. All that was to change.

There were about seventeen mounds on the site and he was to investigate
the fourth. He had the assistance of Mrs Pretty's gardener and gamekeeper,
and soon they were beginning to dig a narrow trench into the east end of
the mound. It was slow work, for the sandy soil was constantly threatening
to engulf them.

*11 May. About mid-day Jacobs called out he had found a piece of
iron. I immediately stopped the work and carefully explored the area
with a small trowel and uncovered five rivets in position on what
turned out to be the bow of a ship.*

Sutton Hoo in 2008. For the moment the archaeologists have gone
and the tourists have replaced them.

It was at this point that the genius of Brown becomes clear, because he
realised the iron rivets were from a very old boat, and he had seen the rivets
from the 1862 Snape boat in Aldeburgh Museum. He correctly assumed he
was dealing with an Anglo-Saxon boat, which was an extraordinary leap
of imagination as almost none had been found in England. He brilliantly
appreciated that the traditional way of excavating, where a trench is
extended and widened in a carefully planned way, would destroy whatever
evidence was waiting for him. If he had found an ancient vessel – and it was
a very big 'if' – then the size and shape of it had to be recreated with infinite
care. He decided to follow the line of the rivets – to ignore his original
trench – and let them dictate the scale of the excavation. In the intervening
years the chorus of admiration from his peers has shown how fortunate
Mrs Pretty was to employ him.

A boat does not have straight sides like a house. It gracefully curves in
both planes, and the rivets were therefore not going to be easy to follow.
As Brown did not know the size of the boat he was digging, he had no
idea of scale as he located rivets – so he left every one where he found it.

Gradually the brown, rusty lumps of iron began to follow a discernible shape, but it was so enormous he doubted if it was possible. There was no wood planking to guide him, of course; that had all been eaten away in the intervening centuries. Instead he noticed that the sandy soil was a darker colour where the wood had once been, and he worked to that, gently removing soil from within the boat until he came upon the signs of timber and the regularly spaced rivets.

Throughout May 1939, Brown and his helpers skilfully revealed more and more of the boat they had found. By this time he knew he was working in the largest Anglo-Saxon boat found anywhere in Europe. Distinguished archaeologists had begun to visit the site, for word of the extraordinary discovery was spreading throughout their community. On 6th June, Charles Phillips of Selwyn College, Cambridge, came to the site with Mrs Pretty and was simply overwhelmed by what he saw. He immediately informed the British Museum and was subsequently appointed to take charge of

THE RIVER DEBEN AT RENDLESHAM WAS WIDER IN THE DAYS OF THE ANGLO-SAXONS. THE TOWER OF THE CHURCH OF ST GREGORY MAY STAND ON THE SITE OF RAEDWALD'S PALACE.

what would be a momentous task – and all the while the prospect of war inched ever closer!

By 10th July, Phillips had assumed command and brought in his own team of experts. Brown was relegated to the role of rather minor assistant, a situation which caused much annoyance and unease and took many years to forget. It is possible that it was only Mrs Pretty's insistence that enabled him to continue working on site.

As Phillips and his team worked to define the shape and size of the vessel, they became increasingly excited by the evidence emerging in the very centre. There had been a burial chamber erected and it had collapsed in due course, leaving only confusion in the sand. Previous mounds dug by Brown had shown that centuries ago grave robbers had pillaged all of them, and it was assumed that would be repeated here. But there had been no robbers – it was clear that the burial chamber would be intact, a prospect of such stupendous importance that everyone on site admitted to being both nervous and excited at the same time! Contemporary photographs show fabulous treasures such as the purse lid and gold buckle still in the soil, their complex surfaces catching the daylight for the first time in over a thousand years.

As the experts trowelled and brushed their way across the floor of the central burial chamber they uncovered objects which would change the historians' view of the Anglo-Saxons. Within ten days they had revealed the wonders of a lost royal dynasty, harking back to its past, for some of the most valuable items may have been brought over from Sweden.

Day after day the boat gave up its secrets: there were warlike artefacts – a sword, helmet, spears, chain mail and a massive gold-leafed shield. The great standard and the whetstone proclaimed the status of the grave's occupant. Although the body of the dead leader had long ago been erased by the acids in the soil, the personal jewellery traced where it had once lain: the purse was attached to a belt secured with the gold belt buckle. An intricate series of buckles, all of gold and beautifully decorated, showed how the weight of the sword and scabbard was distributed. The cloak would have been held in place by two pairs of exquisitely worked gold clasps, displaying coloured *millefiori* glass in the panels. The effect is stunning, and they are unique to Sutton Hoo.

There was also evidence of the belief that a journey was about to take place, for a meal had been placed on the great silver dish and around it

PERHAPS THE SYMBOL OF THE ANGLO-SAXON NATION – THE MAGNIFICENT
HELMET FROM SUTTON HOO. (*British Museum*)

THE GREAT GOLD BELT BUCKLE FROM SUTTON HOO. THE ANGLO-SAXONS DELIGHTED IN INTRICATE DESIGNS. THERE ARE 13 ANIMALS TO BE FOUND HERE! (*British Museum*)

were many other bowls and plates. There was particular interest directed towards a pair of silver spoons bearing the names Saul and Paul, for it was reasoned they were likely to be baptismal. At the feet were two drinking horns and six maplewood bottles.

The burial chamber was cleared by the end of July, its unique and priceless objects filling the hastily gathered boxes and bags which had been collected to hold them. The moss which covered part of the site was found to be perfect as wadding. For several days the boxes were stored beneath the bed of Mrs Pretty!

One of the excavators, Ward-Perkins, was struck by one aspect in particular: 'There's something very fascinating about gold. It comes out of the earth just as it went in. It is still bright and shining and to dust the sand off, and to see the gold with this pattern coming out amongst the sand is an experience which personally I shall never forget.'

The great gold buckle was so perfectly preserved that the spring which operated the lid on the back of the buckle worked first time!

On 31st July all 263 treasures from Sutton Hoo were conveyed to the British Museum, every precaution having been made for their security.

Unfortunately, one small matter was overlooked – the van ran out of petrol and had to be pushed through the gates of the museum!

Phillips was now able to turn his thoughts to the business of writing up the account of the excavation and reaching conclusions about the artefacts as the various bits were cleaned and restored. He spent some time studying the boat's outline and reached the conclusion that, at the time of its burial, it was quite old, for such was the excellence of Brown's work that it was possible to see where planks had been repaired. The tholes, which restrain the oars, were also visible as dark shades in the soil – an extraordinary testament to the skill with which the team had uncovered the boat.

The treasure trove inquest took place in Sutton village hall on 14th August before Mr L.H. Vulliamy. He heard the various statements given by Mrs Pretty, Basil Brown, Charles Phillips and a few others, and then allowed the jury of fourteen men to reach the only sensible conclusion: it was not treasure trove (as the original owner had intended to return for

THE SUTTON HOO INQUEST ESTABLISHED THAT MRS EDITH PRETTY WAS THE LEGAL OWNER OF THE FABULOUS SHIP BURIAL TREASURES.

SUFFOLK SHIP – BURIAL FINDS NOT TREASURE TROVE

JURY'S FINDING AT SUTTON INQUEST

EXPERT ON RITES AT CHIEF'S FUNERAL

SHIP SHOWED SIGNS OF USE

The rich hoard of gold and silver ornaments and vessels and other precious objects recovered from the great Anglo-Saxon ship buried at Sutton Hoo is not "treasure trove."

This was the verdict of the jury at the inquest held on the treasure at Sutton Village Hall, yesterday. The jury also declared that Mrs. E. M. Pretty on whose estate the discovery was made, who was responsible for the excavations being commenced and had defrayed the cost of labour, was the finder

were the first objects discovered. They were found about July 18th and she described how from then onwards other articles were unearthed. When work was suspended for a day or two she arranged to have a police guard all the time until the valuables had been recovered. The police guard was also provided at her expense.

Mr. Charles William Phillips, Fellow of Selwyn College, Cambridge, who said that he was in charge of the opening of the tumulus since July 8th, handed to the Coroner a two-page typewritten list of the gold and silver articles found in the burial ship.

He said that he was not sure whether the forty gold coins were used for payment or exchange, because they were not really coins. They were all copies of older gold coins of the Roman and Byzantine Empires bearing the heads of Roman and Byzantine Emperors. They were less than a quarter of an inch in diameter.

When the Coroner asked what was the object of having copies of older coins, Mr. Phillips said that he could not answer the question, except to say that it might have been done in order to have it), and so it belonged to Mrs Pretty. Overnight she became a millionaire, but within a week she had donated everything to the British Museum as a gift. Prime Minister Winston Churchill would later offer her the honour of Dame of the British Empire, but she turned it down. She died in 1942, so never saw the treasure displayed in the British Museum.

Although the Sutton Hoo mound may have yielded up its secrets, perhaps the greatest treasure it yielded was not formed of gold or silver but it has nevertheless survived as long, and has spread around the world – the English language. It is an exciting, wonderful prospect.

To help them endure the long dark winter evenings, the Anglo-Saxons told stories of their greatest heroes, some from the very dawn of time. These tales were not originally written down, of course, but recited from memory by the poet, who was endowed with priest-like status. The finest of these stories was the tale of *Beowulf* – a warrior who fought and triumphed over hideous, cruel monsters, and was at last, in his old age, killed while recovering treasure from a dragon's lair.

Many scholars believe the story was first told in East Anglia, and at the

THE STORY OF SUTTON HOO IS WELL TOLD IN THE EXHIBITION HALL, WHICH INCLUDES A FULL SIZE REPLICA OF THE BURIAL CHAMBER.

A RECONSTRUCTION OF THE BURIAL CHAMBER AT SUTTON HOO BY ELIZABETH MITCHELS. ALL OF THE TREASURES SURVIVED, BUT RAEDWALD'S BODY HAD DISAPPEARED.

time of Raedwald's burial. There are even people who wonder whether the poet was inspired by the funeral he had personally witnessed at Sutton Hoo. The poet speaks of wild boars above the eye-sockets of the helmet mask. For years scholars assumed this was the fruit of his imagination, but the helmet found at Sutton Hoo displays them as they are described:

> *The head was encircled by a silver helmet which was*
> *As perfect as when the weapon-smith had wonderfully made it*
> *So that no sword should afterward be able to cut through*
> *The defending wild boars that faced about it.*
>
> *(translated: Michael Alexander)*

Within the grave the poet exactly places the objects found on Mrs Pretty's estate – helmet, sword, shield, standard and even a lyre. The hoard of fiction has become the fabulous treasure of fact!

King Sabert & Queen Baldehildis

oad widening schemes often provide archaeologists with their first clues, and so it was in the case of Prittlewell, to the north of Southend-on-Sea, in Essex. Once the road plans had been drawn up, it was standard procedure for the Museum of London to be invited to evaluate the site before the earth-moving machines arrived.

On 23rd October 2003, Ian Blair had been digging for just one day when he came across evidence of a large square of disturbed soil, from which poked the tell-tale green of a copper bowl. What quickened his pulse was the revelation that one of the handle rings was still hanging from an iron hook in the wall. He soon uncovered a tomb with a timber floor and sides which was extraordinarily well preserved. 'The chamber was intact and undisturbed, with items still on the walls where they were hung 1,400 years ago,' said Blair, who went on to explain that because the sand had gently seeped into the chamber there had been no sudden collapse of the roof, and the air had been forced out, which greatly aided preservation.

Gradually, the full extent of what he had found became clear. In a chamber 4 metres square and 1.5 metres high was the grave of a king of the East Saxons who had died at about the same time as Raedwald at Sutton Hoo. Four copper bowls were still hanging where they had been placed and wherever one looked could be seen gold, silver, copper and iron. David Miles, the Chief Archaeologist at English Heritage, said: 'This is a discovery of international importance, which stunningly illuminates the rich and complex world of the so-called Dark Ages.'

Within the chamber was a coffin, in which a body had been placed, although, owing to the acidic nature of the soil, only a tooth survived. Shoe

ARCHAEOLOGISTS FROM THE MUSEUM OF LONDON AT WORK IN THE PRITTLEWELL BURIAL CHAMBER. A BOWL CAN BE SEEN "HANGING ON THE WALL" AT THE BACK. (*Museum of London*)

buckles alone indicated where the feet had been, and they were pointing to the east, a Christian practice. The dead man had been dressed simply and without all the trappings of treasure which might be expected, although this did not prevent the media calling him 'The King of Bling'.

Who was the king? A key factor in the probable identification was the number of artefacts with specifically Christian associations. In the coffin were two tiny gold foil crosses, which might have been placed over the eyes. In the chamber itself was a spoon which was very worn and damaged, suggesting it had been in constant use. It had an illegible Latin inscription on it, and perhaps a cross as well. A cast bronze flagon, which had been found hanging from the plank wall, originally came from Turkey. It may once have been used for the ritual washing of feet. The lid of the flagon was attached to the handle by a chain, and around the neck were three panels showing saints on horseback.

All of these objects confirmed the dead king had embraced the religion of Rome. In AD 604, the East Saxon king, Sabert, had converted to Christianity, persuaded by his uncle Ethelbert of Kent. Raedwald had converted – albeit briefly – at the same time. Sabert died in 616, and the general evidence of dating makes him the most likely candidate for the Prittlewell burial.

In the chamber were a sword and shield, and also a great iron standard – all indicative of a leader's grave. There were also items of great beauty, like two pairs of glass vessels in blue and green glass. They are decorated with petals which hang from wavy lines and bear witness to the craftsmanship which created them. Two drinking horns were identified, and in all such graves they indicate a person of the highest status. One of the copper cauldrons was an astonishing 75 cms in diameter.

Included in the 140 items recovered were objects to entertain the king in the afterlife. A dark stain in the sand was shown to have been a lyre, with silver, copper and iron fittings. The evidence was sufficient for a replica to be constructed. There were also 57 gaming pieces, made from the ball joints of animal leg bones, and a pair of dice, made from an antler. An iron folding chair, also from Turkey, was particularly interesting as it is a unique find in Britain at this time. It may have been a gift.

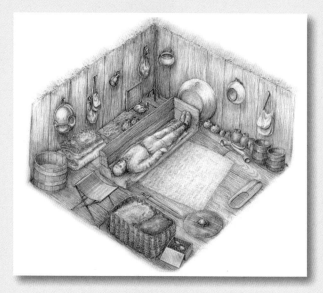

A RECONSTRUCTION OF THE PRITTLEWELL BURIAL CHAMBER BY FAITH VARDY, SHOWING THE ARRANGEMENT OF GRAVE GOODS AS THEY WERE FOUND. (*Museum of London*)

CAISTOR ST EDMUND WAS A ROMAN TOWN, KNOWN AS VENTA ICENORUM, ('MARKET PLACE OF THE ICENI') ONLY THE WALLS SURVIVE. THE HARFORD FARM BROOCH WAS FOUND CLOSE BY.

The excavation was completed by the end of December 2003, and the coroner subsequently ruled that all the items belonged to Southend Borough Council. In the course of time the treasure may be exhibited in Southend and at the Museum of London. These very early years of the 'Dark Ages' can only be glimpsed occasionally, and then imperfectly. In 1905 a lady of leisure called Nina Layard excavated almost 200 graves at Hadleigh Road, west of Ipswich. They dated from AD 550–640. Many were of the wealthy, as shown by the quality of their brooches and necklaces, and others were of soldiers, buried with spears, shields and knives. None of the dead seemed to have been killed in battle; so the graveyard was a final resting place for the first townsfolk of Ipswich. Nina Layard became such an expert on the site that she was honoured by the Society of Antiquaries, which invited her to write a report for their London conference. She was less impressed when they insisted it be read by a man, as women were not permitted to speak!

The Anglo-Saxons did not build in stone or live in great cities. As they surveyed the Roman ruins which were evident all around them, they could not imagine how fellow human beings could have created them. They spoke of roads and city walls as being 'the cunning work of giants'. They may not have moved inside the city fortifications at first, but they no doubt appreciated the river crossings and quaysides. At Caistor St Edmund, near

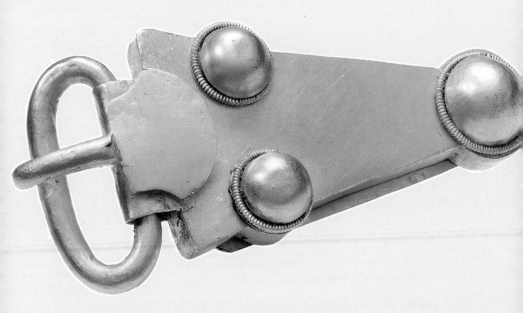

THE GOLD BELT BUCKLE FROM THE PRITTLEWELL EXCAVATION DATING FROM THE FIRST HALF OF THE 7TH CENTURY. (*Museum of London*)

Norwich, was the old city of Venta Icenorum, and continuity of settlement is suggested by the remarkable discovery of a brooch during the construction in 1989 of a new ring road.

The Harford Farm brooch is an object of great beauty, dating from the first half of the 7th century, but it may also illuminate a more gentle side of the new East Anglians. It is a gold pendant, designed to hang from a chain about the neck, and it has been reset with Roman intaglio – a technique where the image is incised below the surface. It is inlaid with garnets – semi-precious stones set in spaces formed by strips of gold wire. This is a possession of someone who was fabulously rich and important. Along with the brooch there was other jewellery, including a silver chain and other gold pendants, besides a toilet set.

Even as a piece of jewellery, the Harford brooch is exceptional, which explains the value of £91,000 Norwich Castle Museum had to find to keep it. But it also has a runic inscription – a form of very simple writing used by the first English invaders. The message is 'May Luda make amends by means of this brooch'. Was it a peace offering from Luda to his wife or sweetheart?

It was in AD 640 that a young girl from the south of England was seized and carried off to France as a slave. Her name was Baldehildis, and she was sold into the household of Erchinoald, the chief minister to Clovis II, king of all the Franks. Her exceptional beauty and intelligence soon worked in her favour, for within a few years she had married the king and become his queen! Although King Clovis died only a few years later, Baldehildis' astonishing career was far from over. She became regent for her son and remained at the very centre of French affairs for several more years. Not surprisingly, during her regency she worked to end the slave trade and became a great friend and ally of the Church. Her good works made her name famous throughout France, and she was an important benefactress of many religious houses, including the convent of Chelles, near Paris. Eventually, in 665, court politics and the ambition of her son caught up with this extraordinary lady and she was obliged to retire to a nunnery at Chelle, where she died in 680. Such was her reputation for charity and goodness that in due course she was canonised, and entered the medieval pantheon of worthy female saints.

Finding any object with a name on it is obviously an additional thrill for a metal detectorist, but finding one with a famous name is doubly rewarding. Mr Crawford was working an area near Postwick, east of Norwich, in April 1998 when he picked up a clear signal beneath the ground at his feet. Once he had cleared away the soil he discovered a tiny gold object which resembled a coin, and a small one at that, for it was just 1 cm in diameter. It was obviously very old, and he took it to the museum to find out more about it.

Immediately there was a quickening of interest, for he had found a 7th-century gold swivel-bezel seal matrix. It had once been mounted in a signet ring but that had been lost. The seal matrix was used to press the design into hot wax and so seal letters and documents. This particular seal was able to swivel, allowing it to offer two different designs depending on the sender's choice. The swivel bar still runs through the centre. The gold double-sided seal was unique, but what made it completely astonishing was the name inscribed on one of its sides – Baldehildis.

There is a face which could be Jesus, or it could be Woden, such is the lack of detail. Above the head is a simple Christian cross. As a seal it would

ORIGINALLY PART OF A FINGER RING, THIS GOLD, DOUBLE-SIDED SEAL MATRIX, MADE ABOUT 1350 YEARS AGO, WAS USED FOR PRESSING A PATTERN IN WAX TO SEAL DOCUMENTS. (*Norwich Castle Museum*)

have been quite acceptable, but the design on the back may have required a bit more discretion. It shows a couple making love, or at the very least, embracing. She has long, flowing hair, he is touching her intimately, and neither seems to be wearing any clothes. The most likely explanation for the double-sided seal matrix has to be that one side was for official business, and the other was a very personal token. Was the whole seal a fertility gift? What if it was only ever supposed to have been used by a husband and wife? What are the chances that it once belonged to Queen Baldehildis? How did it come to be found in Norfolk?

Obviously, there is little hope of the truth being known, but seals like this were only to be found in the possession of the super rich, which limits the number of likely owners. Suppose that the queen was as beautiful as the chronicles say, and that she used the ring to communicate with a lover – or her husband! When she entered the convent she would have appreciated that the ring seal was now inappropriate, and it is quite possible she could have given the seal and ring to a trusted servant, or perhaps it was just stolen. However it did so, it returned to England, where it was lost in a Norfolk field for well over a thousand years. When it next saw the daylight it was valued at £60,000 and ended up in a cabinet in the Norwich Castle Museum.

THE VIKING ONSLAUGHT

Tony Langwith was a metal detectorist who liked to combine his hobby with a bit of fishing. In 1978 he was with his nephew beside the river Little Ouse at Brandon, and he idly scanned the ground of the river bank. Suddenly, he received a strong signal, and no more than two inches below the ground he uncovered something that he knew was gold.

For the moment it looked like part of a block of sand, but he knew how to find out more: he took it to the curator of Norwich Museum who identified it as being an Anglo-Saxon gold plaque of the sort which may have decorated the cover of a large, illuminated bible. Much later, when it had been restored and written up, Sotheby's valued it at £14,000 and Mr Langwith's afternoon's fishing had turned a nice profit. The plaque is now in the British Museum.

The gold plaque dates from the first decades of the 9th century, when Brandon was a minster on the edge of the flood plain. It had been founded in the 7th century and its community of monks was responsible for preaching and taking services in the surrounding villages and towns. Their handwritten bibles were the glory of this period and they were beautiful works of art in their own right, complete with gorgeous covers. There would once have been a large church at Brandon, and excavation has shown that once there were as many as 35 buildings, as well as two cemeteries. Brandon itself was attached to the much larger community at Ely, which had been founded by St Etheldreda, a Wuffing princess.

The plaque shows a man – or it is probably a saint – with an eagle's head, dressed in priestly robes and holding a quill pen and a book. The design is inlaid with niello to ensure it stands out. His halo is very evident, and his identity is apparent from the Latin inscription: St John the Evangelist. The eagle is the symbol of St John, as are the book and pen, so it is most likely this was attached to a bible cover, using the holes in the corners. If it was a complete New Testament, then there are still the plaques to Matthew, Mark and Luke to be located.

The Viking onslaught on East Anglia commenced in AD 841. At first they attacked, and then allowed themselves to be bought off. These new foes were fiercer than any others encountered and although brutal and seemingly invincible they were also magnificent ship-builders and mariners.

The martyrdom of King Edmund in AD 869 is one of the most important moments of East Anglian history, and yet the site remains unknown, as does the man himself. Traditionally, Edmund had been king of the East Angles for no more than three years when he faced his greatest challenge. He is said to have brought his army against the Danes at a place called 'Haegelisdun' – which may be Hoxne – where, as a Christian, he refused to shed the blood of his enemies. They had no such quibbles and reputedly tied him to a tree and fired arrows into his body. After such a death the crown of martyrdom was his, and, when in AD 902, his body was interred in the abbey at Beodricsworth, it was inevitable the name of this place would be changed to Bury St Edmunds to reflect its association with St Edmund. With the loss of their king, the people of East Anglia made their peace with the Danes, who now turned their thoughts to settlement and trade.

Part of East Anglia was conquered by Edward the Elder in AD 917, when someone buried a hoard of 90 coins at Brantham in Suffolk, overlooking the river Stour estuary. They were found in 2002. Sometimes place-names provide a clue to a moment in the past. 'Brantham' recalls the time the Danes attacked and burnt the settlement in 911, for it means 'burnt hamlet'.

There are other finds from this era. In 1977 William King, a gravedigger in the Norfolk village of Pentney, was hard at work with his spade when he came across six Anglo-Saxon brooches, all in excellent condition. Unaware of the significance of what he had found, he handed them to the vicar, who locked them in the vestry and thought no more about them. The brooches were only re-discovered when the Revd John Wilson took over the parish three years later, and he thought them worth investigating. He sent them up to the British Museum, which informed him that they were from the 9th century and 'among the most intricate and finely-wrought pieces of

THIS PHOTOGRAPH SHOWS THE TRENCH DUG BY THE BUILDERS IN THE
GROUNDS OF WYMONDHAM COLLEGE AT MORLEY ST PETER.
(Norwich Castle Museum)

late Saxon metalwork, and of national importance'. William King, had
probably forgotten about the things he had found, but presumably he was
more than grateful for the £135,000 which he received when the museum
bought them from him.

In Ipswich Museum there is a lovely silver pendant showing a warrior
holding a sword and shield. It was found at Wickham Market in 2002 and
had been created by a Danish craftsman in the late 9th century. The figure
is wearing a long tunic. Incidentally, this illustrates the problems which
occurred when English and Norse collided – they had their own words for
such things. In English the tunic is a *shirt*, whereas in Norse it is a *skirt*.

Bob Spall was a metal detectorist who kept finding coins in a field
at Ashdon in Essex. By 1984 he had dug up twelve silver coins, seven
fragments of coins and many more isolated bits of coins. But these were
not just any coins – they were Danish forgeries! Quite deliberately someone
in about AD 890–895 had set out to copy the coins of the English king,
Alfred the Great. From the moment they arrived in England the Danish
conquerors found themselves assimilating the way of life they found. Apart
from language, they needed to trade with neighbours, and that could mean

moving across the ill-defined frontiers. They soon came to understand the value of money and while they had little experience of it in their own past they recognized how useful it could be – so they imitated Alfred's. A dozen coins demonstrate that, when it made good sense, Danes and English were able to come to terms with each other's different customs!

The discovery of Norfolk's largest hoard of Anglo-Saxon coins was, in a way, all the fault of the snow. In 1958 Wymondham College in Norfolk was preparing to build a new boarding house, and before the bricklayers could get down to work, the drains had to be dug underneath. Friday, 24th January was a freezing cold day, and two men called Bird and Hervey were looking forward to the weekend and a respite from the finger-chilling temperatures. By the end of the afternoon they were working in a snowstorm, and, as fast as they cut the trench, it was lost beneath a blanket of white invisibility. They eagerly packed away their tools and left, wondering what it would look like when they returned.

Monday was much better. Most of the snow had gone, and that was how they noticed something odd: as it melted, the snow had caused the trench to collapse and so exposed a dull grey earthenware jar, from which a few coins had fallen. The more they looked, the more coins they saw, so they went to the college and told them about it, and eventually an archaeologist came out to inspect their find. Nothing is ever secret for long in a school, and by the time the experts arrived the pupils had sieved more soil and found a further nine coins.

When the trench had been fully explored, a grand total of 883 silver coins had been found. All but one had been minted during the reigns of Alfred the Great and his son, Edward the Elder. A single coin from the reign of Athelstan suggested an approximate date of AD 924, which was particularly interesting as it may mean that the coins had been hidden – for whatever reason – at just the time when the kings of Wessex were making themselves all-powerful throughout southern England by warfare and treaty. An indication of the value of such a hoard is that the owner could have used it to buy 29 oxen or 176 sheep!

When the coroner's inquest took place at Wymondham College it was only concerned with the silver coins, and not the Thetford-ware jar in which they were found, because that was not classified as treasure (after the important change to the law in 1996 the humble pot would also qualify as treasure). 'Norfolk men share £2,700 treasure trove reward,' proclaimed the newspaper, and so they did. One of them sold his caravan and bought a house instead. As for the coins, the British Museum took the best, and Norwich Castle Museum has a very fine display, including the jar. Wymondham College still has six of the coins to show for its trouble, and if things ever get tough they can always exchange them for a sheep!

Although East Anglia had been brought back into the Anglo-Saxon fold, and looked to Winchester or London for its king, the Danes remained an intermittent threat, periodically devastating towns and cities around the coast. For 30 years they were the royal family of England! As we have seen,

IN 1958 A HOARD OF ANGLO-SAXON COINS WAS DISCOVERED AT
WYMONDHAM COLLEGE. IT HAD BEEN BURIED IN A JAR IN ABOUT AD 924.
(*Norwich Castle Museum*)

at such times wealthy people buried their goods in the hope of more peaceful times to follow. Not all of them were reunited with their property.

In 1687 at Hundon, Suffolk, a sexton digging a grave in the churchyard came upon almost 300 silver pennies from the reigns of Athelstan, Edmund and Eadred. Unfortunately, he sold the coins to two local antiquarians and nothing remains beyond the fact of their discovery. Assuming the identification of the coins was accurate, the hoard dated from the middle of the 10th century.

Ipswich was an attractive prize for roaming Danish fleets and in AD 983 the town was attacked twice. The panic caused as the ships nosed their way up the Orwell must have been terrible, and doubtless a great deal of value was hastily buried in gardens or under barn floors. During work in the town's Buttermarket in 1863 about 500 silver pennies were found, all in excellent condition. Of all the people who buried their property at that time, one at least did not return for it. The raids continued and, in AD 991, Ipswich was once again sacked before the Danish ships moved into the Blackwater estuary, where they inflicted a massive defeat at the fateful battle of Maldon.

By the evening of 14th October 1066, the Anglo-Saxon age had ended, crushed on the field at Hastings by a ruthless opportunist who ventured everything on a single battle, and won a kingdom as a result. As the Norman lords, with names like Clare, Bigod, de Vere and Malet rode into East Anglia to take possession of their rewards did they worry that the people would bury all their gold and silver to keep it from them? The archaeology suggests it rarely happened, but that is not the same as never.

At Campsea Ash, Suffolk, in 1832, over 600 coins were discovered. Edward the Confessor is well represented, but many show the head of Harold II, who reigned only from January to October 1066, so they are incredibly rare. The coins were found in two lead cases, and it is not too fanciful to imagine an Englishman placing them in the ground before he gathered up his weapons and set off to serve his king at Hastings. He would be one of thousands who did not return from that most famous of battlefields. The Norman Conquest would be no mere disruption, to be followed in time by a return to the old ways. From the first it was apparent that the Normans were here to stay. England, and the English, would never be the same again.

TREASURES LOST & FOUND

ike Seager and Andy Slinn were metal detectorists and, in April 1999, they were investigating a ploughed field near Thwaite in Suffolk. When they picked up a signal and subsequently uncovered a small metallic object, they contacted the county finds liaison officer, who came out and took it away. What they had found was a medieval silver gilt lid from a reliquary cross, and it was extremely rare.

In an age of faith, people believed that objects associated with saints were able to help and protect them, so they kept them as personal items of jewellery, like crosses. The Thwaite Cross was very small, only 77 mm long and 45.5 mm high, but it was made of silver and may once have hung round the owner's neck.

After cleaning, the cross was shown to be an image of the crucified Christ with a halo. His arms are outstretched and above his head are the hands of God. The actual container for the relic is missing, only the lid survives. In all probability it originated in Denmark, as it matches examples from that country, and the late 11th-century date makes it possible to imagine that it was brought to England by a Norman after the Conquest. At Southwold in November 1999, the coroner declared it to be treasure, and the finders received the sum of £1,500 from the British Museum, which now possesses it.

When Arthur Davey's young son went to infants' school and tried to swap a doll for a toy car he was disappointed that there were no takers. His father had found the doll while ploughing at Rattlesden in 1971, and, even after it had been cleaned, young Davey would have preferred the car. Later a friend of the family saw the doll on the mantelpiece and suggested that it might be worth having it examined by an expert, as occasionally fields do produce unusual finds.

When Ipswich Museum saw it, there was great interest: the doll was a gilt bronze statuette of St John the Evangelist and it was made in the late 12th century. At Christie's auction rooms in December 1972 it sold for £36,750, and Arthur Davey could only be grateful that his son's school friend had chosen to hang on to his toy car!

Of course, not all treasure has yet been found. Sometimes the legend of fabulous wealth hidden beneath the ground is enough to set the pulse racing, and in East Anglia the story of how King John lost his treasure when the waves of the Wash swept over his baggage wagons is one of the most popular. To this day there are people searching for the find of a lifetime. But there is only one fact, and that is that King John lost it on 12th October 1216.

The background is easily explained: John taxed his English subjects so harshly that the barons rebelled and forced him to sign Magna Carta in 1215, by which he promised not to do so again. Less than a year later the king believed he was strong enough to break his word and set out to

THIS GILT-BRONZE STATUETTE OF ST JOHN THE EVANGELIST DATES FROM THE LATE 12TH CENTURY. IT WAS ONCE PART OF AN ALTAR CROSS WHICH ALSO INCLUDED IMAGES OF CHRIST AND THE VIRGIN MARY. (*Ipswich Museum*)

deal with the barons who had humiliated him. In October 1216 John was at King's Lynn, planning a campaign in Lincolnshire. Although suffering from dysentery, he ignored advice to rest and set off for Swineshead, near Sleaford, on the other side of the Wash, intending to reach it by the end of the day. He went via Wisbech. It was a 40-mile journey across difficult country, but the real problem was how to move all his baggage wagons and the large numbers of people who travelled with him, perhaps as many as two thousand.

The solution was to send them by a shorter route. While John and his personal escort went south before heading towards Swineshead, the slow moving, cumbersome wagons, guarded by soldiers, would use the trackway which crossed the Wellstream from Walpole Cross Keys to Sutton St Mary. This was a much shorter distance, requiring only that the whole convoy be back on high ground before the tide swept over the causeway. John arrived at Swineshead Abbey on the evening of 12th October and awaited his baggage, which included his coronation regalia and all the money needed to pay his troops.

Late that evening John learnt the extent of the disaster. An unexpected change in the tide had caught his wagons as they slowly made their way across an estuary track and now they were all gone. Or were they? Ever since, there have been arguments about what was lost and where. Clearly a great deal of value was missing, and the campaign was all but over, but the prospect of the crown jewels being found today in the muddy pools of the Wash is doubtful. Even if they had fallen victim to the sea, they may have been 'rescued' by local people who knew their tide tables! When Henry III was crowned soon afterwards, there were no crown jewels used, which suggests that they had been lost, but at his formal coronation in 1220 he appears to have been decked out in all of them! Quite simply, we shall never know what happened. The lovely cup on display in King's Lynn rejoices in the name King John's Cup, and might have been the only survivor of the loss had it not been made at least a century later!

Sometimes archaeology can show us an aspect of our history we would prefer to forget. In 1902 labourers were at work building a bank in High Street, Colchester, when they came upon a lead bucket, which was clearly very old. When they looked inside it was found to contain almost 11,000 silver coins, most of them pennies dating from the reign of Henry III. In all probability they were buried in the year 1256 by Jewish moneylenders.

Why might such a large sum be hidden at that time, and why was it not recovered? Events in Lincoln only the year before may provide the answer.

Since the time of their arrival following the Conquest, Jews had always been regarded with suspicion and envy. Christians were forbidden to charge interest on money they lent, whereas Jews had no such restrictions, indeed it was about the only profession open to them. Accordingly, some of them grew very powerful and even kings relied on their support. In 1255 a boy called Hugh was kidnapped and crucified by the Jews in Lincoln – at least that was the story widely believed. Hugh of Lincoln was immediately canonized and given a grand burial in the cathedral. Across the country moneylenders were killed and their property destroyed. It is quite likely that in Colchester the terrible news from Lincoln caused the Jewish community to take precautions.

Just 30 metres from the site of the 1902 discovery, another was made in 1969, in Culver Street. Once again workmen were digging a trench when they found a cache of coins similar to those found in the High Street. They were in such good condition that they were thought to be brand new sixpences. There were 14,000 silver pennies this time, and they were slightly later in date; indeed they crossed into the reign of Edward I, who became king in 1272. The story they illustrated was even darker, for in 1275 Edward decreed that all Jews over seven years old had to wear a badge and remain within their quarters. The repression continued and massacres of Jewish communities occurred across England, often unchecked by the authorities. In such circumstances it is easy to see why a Colchester moneylender in the decade after 1268 might bury his valuables and hope to avoid attention.

Clare, in Suffolk, is a pretty village, which welcomes tourists to its exceptional church and marketplace of timber-frame and thatch buildings. It also has the remains of a great Norman castle, but the mound on which it stood was extensively altered when the Great Eastern Railway decided to build a station yard there in 1865. One of the workers was William Lorking, described as 'a poor village lad', who announced that his spade had uncovered something unexpected.

He had found a gold crucifix, studded with pearls and showing an image of Christ. Attached to it was a 2 ft long gold neck-chain. Scholarly investigation revealed it to have once been the property of Lionel, Duke of Clarence, King Edward III's son. He was said to have given it to his daughter, Philippa, who had lived at Clare castle. News of such a heartwarming discovery eventually reached the ears of Queen Victoria herself, who let it be known that she would like it *back*. Her claim to a Plantagenet jewel would always be tenuous in the extreme! The railway company, keen to proclaim their loyalty, kindly presented Her Majesty with the heirloom, and she graciously rewarded William Lorking with three gold sovereigns. It is not known where his coins are now, but the cross may be admired in the British Museum.

It will be a sad day when the myths and legends of the past are excluded from history simply because they cannot be proved. East Anglia has several such oral treasures, and the tale of the Pedlar of Swaffham is one of them.

Once upon a time in Swaffham there lived a pedlar. Now it happened that one night, as he slept, he dreamed that if he stood upon London Bridge he would hear wonderful news. In the morning he thought about his dream but decided to ignore it and stay at home. But on two further nights he had the same dream and so, full of curiosity, he set out for the great city. Standing on the bridge, he recognized the shops from his dream and wondered what would happen next. After two or three days standing in the same place he was ready to give up and return to Swaffham.

At that moment a shopkeeper, who had noticed the pedlar, came over and asked him why he stood there for so long. Upon being told that the pedlar had come in search of wonderful news, the shopkeeper burst out laughing, saying: 'What a pair we are! I too have had dreams. Mine told me to go into Norfolk, to a town called Swaffham, where I should find a treasure buried beneath a large tree in the garden of a pedlar. I am not such a fool as to heed such nonsense and neither should you.'

At this the pedlar experienced great excitement and hastened back home, where he dug beneath the tree in his garden, and found a vast hoard of treasure, which transformed his fortunes, making him a generous and respected member of the town.

Stories such as this are to be found across England, and they are hard to substantiate. However, in this case, church records do show that a pedlar called John Chapman did live in Swaffham, where he later became a merchant and churchwarden, and that in 1462 he made generous bequests to the church. In the choir there are two carved stalls: one showing the pedlar with a great pack on his back, and the other of him and his wife (and dog) looking out from their shop. These were once in his family pew, so they offer a pleasing blend of fact and fiction.

A FINIAL ON A PEW IN THE CHURCH OF ST PETER AND ST PAUL SHOWS THE SWAFFHAM PEDLAR WITH HIS DOG.

AND PEPYS CAME BACK!

All wars are terrible, but perhaps civil wars are the worst. In the 1640s Englishmen stood upon a field of battle and saw against them others from their country, sometimes even from their own family.

To the normal dangers of living through violent times, there was added the attendant lawlessness and destruction inevitable when soldiers roamed through the land, terrorizing whole communities – even when they were ostensibly on the same side. Families with savings in gold and silver needed to know that it was secure, but also that it was readily available to them. The solution was to bury the family fortune in the garden, where it would escape attention. Of all the money hidden in this way, it is not surprising that some was never reclaimed.

Richard and Cherry Fisher of Ashdon, near Saffron Walden, were out walking their dog one day in 1984 when they noticed a coin glinting in soil disturbed by rabbits. They began to search for more and were astonished as the heap grew. A week later they returned to find the rabbits had been at work once more, for there were another 79 coins to be collected. In total they had found well over a thousand silver coins, and while most were of Tudor origin there were a few which reached to 1649 and the year of the king's execution. Here perhaps was a vivid example of the uncertain times produced by the Civil War, in that someone had hidden their wealth while soldiers and desperate strangers roamed the countryside.

West of Ipswich is the village of Washbrook, and here, in 1979, farmer John Faulds of Cole Green Farm was ploughing. He stopped when he glimpsed a coin, and had soon located another thirty. Much later, when the crop had been harvested, he found time to return to the spot and found many more. He ended up with 298 silver coins, once again spanning the

Tudor and Stuart periods, and giving a likely date for burial of 1646. John Faulds received the market value of the coins when they were declared as treasure trove by the coroner.

By 1648 King Charles was a prisoner on the Isle of Wight and the victorious Parliamentary forces assumed the war was over. But the fighting went on as pockets of Royalist resistance broke out and threatened the fragile peace. One such force in Kent was defeated by General Fairfax but it escaped across the Thames into Essex, where it joined the troops of Charles Lucas and Sir George Lisle. This desperate collection of fugitives headed for Colchester and by 12th June 1648 they were asking to be admitted to the town. Lucas was a Colchester man, which proved to be sufficient reason, and the gates were opened, and, when Fairfax and his Parliamentary army arrived and constructed fortifications around the walls, the siege of Colchester had begun. Even to this day the ruins of St Botolph's Priory and the shot holes in the Siege House bear witness to the ferocity of the struggle.

The siege of Colchester was an event all of Essex must have watched and feared. For the villagers of Messing, near Tiptree, it was particularly dangerous as the Parliamentary army passed close by on its way to confront the rebels. The punishments meted out to those who surrendered included being sold into slavery in the West Indies; so the message was clear. A Royalist sympathizer, having endured so many years of danger, must have decided he could delay no longer, and hid his fortune in the ground. In 1975, all 2,223 silver coins were found in the earthenware pot as he had left them.

For all sorts of reasons, Cromwell's republic failed, and, when Charles II was invited back to England in 1660, and the monarchy was restored, there were thousands of people who knew that the time for settling old scores was at hand. Although the only people executed were those who had actually signed King Charles I's death warrant, there were many more who had reason to fear the worst.

One such person lived in an old cottage in Ridgewell, north Essex, and evidently the Restoration did not find him cheering in the street. He put all his money in a black leather pouch, climbed into the loft and hid it among the beams. When Robert Hall, the owner of Little Meadow End Cottage, was working in the loft in 1980 he accidentally put his foot through the floorboards and so found the hoard left there in the dangerous times of

IN THIS GARDEN AT BRAMPTON, SAMUEL PEPYS SEARCHED BY CANDLELIGHT
FOR HIS BURIED TREASURE AND FOUND ALMOST ALL OF IT!

1660. In all, there were 175 silver coins, which included 74 shillings and 79 sixpences, and what made them so unusual was that their dates covered almost two centuries, from 1461 right up to 1625, an impressive generation span for one family.

Samuel Pepys was educated at Huntingdon School and Magdalene College, Cambridge. As a student in 1649 he had enthusiastically witnessed the execution of King Charles I. Understandably, once he was offered a job in the service of King Charles II, he kept very quiet about his behaviour that day! By June 1660 Pepys was Clerk of the Acts to the Navy Board – an Admiralty civil servant – though better known to us as the author of his extraordinary diary.

Wars against Britain's trade rivals, the Dutch, produced some humiliating defeats, and, when in June 1667, the Dutch fleet sailed up the Thames, attacked the naval dockyard in the Medway and carried off *The Royal Charles*, the English flagship, the public bayed for vengeance on those who had allowed it to happen. Pepys was innocent, but that appeared to carry little weight and he feared for his life – and his savings. The family home was at Brampton, outside Huntingdon, and so in June 1667 Pepys sent his gold there in the care of his wife. She had instructions to bury £1,300 in the garden, taking great care that no one should see her doing so.

By October the crisis had passed and Pepys travelled to Brampton to recover his gold.

> *10 Oct 1667: my father and I with a dark lantern, it being now night, into the garden with my wife and there went about our great work to dig up my gold. But Lord, what a tosse I was for some time in, that they could not justly tell where it was… and at last to fear that it was gone; but by and by, poking with a spit, we found it…but good God, to see how sillily they did it, not half a foot under ground and in the sight of the world from a hundred places.*
> (Transcribed by Robert Latham)

So, his wife had forgotten where she buried it! Pepys now had the task of washing the coins, only to discover about £100 was missing:

> *W. Hewer* (Pepys' servant) *and I did all alone, with several pails of water and basins, at last wash the dirt off of the pieces and parted the pieces and the dirt, and then begun to tell* (count)*; and by a note which I had of the value of the whole do find that there was short above 100 pieces, which did make me mad…so W. Hewer and I out again about midnight and there by candlelight did make shift to gather 45 pieces more – and so in and to cleanse them, and by this time it was past 2 in the morning.*

A further search in the morning eventually left him only about £30 short, which he was willing to accept.

The story Pepys told would be familiar to many of the unknown people in this book, who for 2,000 years buried treasure in the earth: he conveyed his valuables to the burial site; he buried them away from the sight of prying eyes; and he had the anxiety of trying to relocate the site when it was safe to do so. Unlike so many though, he came back.

All over East Anglia there are treasures waiting to be found, and every one would tell a story if it could. Only archaeologists can make them speak!

Treasure Trove – What the Law Says

Most of the finds which are the subject of this book were made when the law of Treasure Trove applied. Since the 13th century, a coroner dealing with the discovery of gold or silver asked only one question: was it the original owner's intention to recover it later? If yes – then it was declared to be treasure trove, and belonged to the Crown. If no – it was not treasure trove and the first finder became the new owner.

In practice, the State paid the finder the full value, and the items were taken into a national collection. All of this was swept away by the 1996 Treasure Act.

The Treasure Act 1996

This very brief summary is designed to be informative, but it is not intended to be a substitute for the various official publications and websites. If you think you have found something important and valuable, it is in your interests to follow the rules. If in doubt, contact your local museum or county archaeologist, who will offer advice and help.

When you find something:

Treasure must be reported under the 1996 Treasure Act. Other finds can be reported voluntarily with the Portable Antiquities Scheme: www.finds.org.uk

Make sure you have permission to search:

You are strongly advised to secure the landowner's permission in writing to search. Council property is governed by local bye-laws, and permission must be obtained in advance.

Metal detectorists should join a national organisation:

For more information contact: www.ncmd.co.uk www.newbury.net/fid

Ownership agreements:

It is usual for the finder to split rewards equally with the landowner.

General points:

Metal detecting should only take place on disturbed plough land and not deeper than the depth of the plough. All finds of both treasure and non-treasure should be reported.

INDEX